ISBN 978-1-5282-6953-7
PIBN 10011310

For support please visit www.forgottenbooks.com

COLUMBIA UNIVERSITY

INDO-IRANIAN SERIES

EDITED BY

A. V. WILLIAMS JACKSON

PROFESSOR OF INDO-IRANIAN LANGUAGES
IN COLUMBIA UNIVERSITY

VOLUME V

New York

THE COLUMBIA UNIVERSITY PRESS

1908

SAYINGS OF BUDDHA

THE

ITI-VUTTAKA

A PALI WORK OF THE BUDDHIST CANON

FOR THE FIRST TIME TRANSLATED
WITH AN INTRODUCTION AND NOTES

BY

JUSTIN HARTLEY MOORE, A.M., Ph.D. (Columbia)

INSTRUCTOR IN FRENCH IN THE COLLEGE OF THE CITY OF NEW YORK

NEW YORK

THE COLUMBIA UNIVERSITY PRESS

1908

TO

MY MOTHER

IN REVERENT MEMORY

182318

PREFATORY NOTE

In this book the Sayings, or Logia, of Buddha are translated for the first time into an Occidental language, and it is gratifying that Dr. Moore has accomplished the task of making them generally accessible.

A. V. WILLIAMS JACKSON.

PREFACE

Since 1841, when Friedrich Spiegel published the first European edition of a Pāli text, the interest taken in the life and teachings of Buddha has been keen and marked. Through the labors of Turnour, D'Alwis, Childers, Fausböll, Oldenberg, Hardy, Kern, Davids, and others, steady progress has been made, both in our knowledge of the career of this great Eastern teacher, and in the interpretation of the sacred books of his canon.

Chief among the agencies for the publication of these texts has been and still is the Pāli Text Society of London, under the direction of its scholarly founder and indefatigable worker, T. W. Rhys Davids. Up to its twenty-fifth anniversary in April, 1907, the society published, through the collaboration of many scholars, a total of 46 Buddhist texts in 59 volumes, amounting in all to over 17,000 octavo pages. In contrast with this great number of editions of the texts themselves, the work of translating and commenting upon them has not, however, made equal progress. Despite the translations of Rhys Davids, Oldenberg, Weber, Neumann, and others, along with the labors of many enthusiastic interpreters, the gaps to be filled in translating the canon are wide and many. For this reason almost any comment or argument on any Buddhist topic must inevitably be regarded as only provisional, if not in some cases even premature, until all the texts, together with their native commentaries, shall have been sifted, compared, interpreted, and criticized.

There is an element of the charm of the unknown in translating a book that has not been previously rendered into a Western tongue. For that reason the work of translating the Itivuttaka has been to me a task of much interest, although the undertaking was somewhat like a dive into unfathomed waters.

Before closing these prefatory remarks, I desire to express my thanks for a number of obligations which I owe to friends. In matters of typography and the like I have had throughout the invaluable assistance of Mr. George C. O. Haas, to whom I gladly take this occasion of expressing my sincere thanks for his kindness in so generously putting at my disposal his exceptional acumen in proof-reading.

My friend and fellow-student, Mr. Charles J. Ogden, of Columbia University, has helped me more than once by his brilliant criticism, and Dr. Truman Michelson, among others, has given me willing advice and comment.

But to one above all have I been a constant debtor throughout this task, from its inception to its completion; one who has played the rôle both of kindly guide and rigorous critic, and who has most generously allotted to me a goodly portion of his time, already filled to overflowing with multifarious duties. Pleasant indeed has been the inspiration gained from a long association with and apprenticeship under my friend and teacher, Professor A. V. Williams Jackson.

JUSTIN HARTLEY MOORE.

COLUMBIA UNIVERSITY,
NEW YORK CITY.
May 18, 1908.

TABLE OF CONTENTS

Apte, Dict.	= Practical Sanskrit-English Dictionary, by V. S. Apte (Poona, 1890).
Böhtlingk.	= Sanskrit-Wörterbuch in kürzerer Fassung, by Otto Böhtlingk (St. Petersburg, 1879).
Böhtlingk and Roth.	= Sanskrit-Wörterbuch, by Otto Böhtlingk and Rudolph Roth (St. Petersburg, 1855).
Childers, Pāli Dict.	= Dictionary of Pāli Language, by R. C. Childers (London, 1875).
Clough, Sinh. Dict.	= Sinhalese-English Dictionary, by Rev. Benjamin Clough (Colombo, 1892).
Dhp.	= Dhammapada.
Iti-v.	= Iti-vuttaka.
JAOS.	= Journal of the American Oriental Society.
JPTS.	= Journal of the Pāli Text Society.
JRAS.	= Journal of the Royal Asiatic Society.
Monier Williams, Skt. Dict.	= Sanskrit-English Dictionary, by Sir Monier Williams (Oxford, 1899).
Mrs. Rhys Davids, DhS.	= A Buddhist Manual of Psychological Ethics, a translation of the Dhamma Sanghani, by C. K. F. Rhys Davids (London, 1900).
op. cit.	= (*opus citatum*), the work previously cited.
SBE.	= Sacred Books of the East.
Whitney, Skt. Gram.	= A Sanskrit Grammar, by William Dwight Whitney (Boston, 1889).
ZDMG.	= Zeitschrift der Deutschen Morgenländischen Gesellschaft.

☞ For the best bibliography of general Buddhist works, see A. J. Edmunds, in Journal of the Pāli Text Society, 1903, pp. 1–61.

INTRODUCTION

Title. The title of this translation, 'Sayings of Buddha,' is a free rendering of the corresponding Pāli title, *Iti-vuttaka*. Literally these two words mean 'thus it hath been said' and refer to the fact that they claim to be the authentic Logia of Buddha. This particular phrase, *iti-vuttaka*, is repeated again and again in the course of the text, and its frequent recurrence was the reason for its use as a designation of this collection of Buddha's sayings.

Place in the Buddhist Canon. The *Iti-vuttaka* is one of the canonical books of Buddhism, and is found in the second grand division of the three 'baskets,' or *piṭakas*, of which the canon is composed. The second division is called the *Sutta-piṭaka*, 'basket of religious instruction,' and consists of five *nikāyas*, or 'collections.' In the fifth of these latter, or the so-called *khuddaka-nikāya*, 'collection of brief selections,' there are found fifteen different works of a varied nature. In the fourth place of this collection of the shorter works of the Buddhist canon stands the *Iti-vuttaka*: included with it in this group of fifteen, be it said in passing, are the well-known *Jātakas*, or 'Birth-Stories,' and the beautiful Buddhist anthology called the *Dhammapada*.

Extent of the Text. In size the Iti-vuttaka is one of the shortest of the Buddhist books, although it comprises 125 pages in the edition by Windisch, in the Pāli Text Society Publications, London, 1890. This edition is the only Occidental one, and it furnishes the text on which this translation is based. In this admirable work of Windisch, only about two thirds of each page is taken up by the text proper, the other third being taken up by the editor's summary of the variant readings.

Arrangement of the Iti-vuttaka. The entire work is divided into one hundred and twelve sections, each partly in prose and

partly in verse. There is also a further arrangement into parts,
. *nipātas,* which are, in their turn, subdivided into chapters, *vaggas.*
As this latter arrangement is of no practical service to the modern
reader, I have for the most part ignored it, merely including
in the translation the headings of these so-called parts and divisions. When a reference is made, therefore, to a word in any
portion of the book, I have given the section number, and to indicate the line in which the particular word occurs, I have ap-
pended a figure, 1, 2, 3, etc., if the word be in the prose portion
of the section, or have affixed a small letter, a, b, c, etc., if the
word be in the poetical part of the section.

Age and Authorship. The date of the Iti-vuttaka is a matter
of extreme uncertainty. According to native tradition, the entire
Buddhist canon was settled definitely at the first great convention
at Rājagaha, shortly after the death of Buddha. No less an
authority than the famous Buddhaghosa repeats this statement
in his introduction to the Sumangala Vilāsini, his commentary on
the Dīgha Nikāya. The twenty-five pages of his introduction,
of which I have a translation under way, give an account of the
composition of the whole Buddhist canon. But it must be re-
membered that Buddhaghosa lived toward the end of the fourth
century A. D., and his views may have to be taken with some
qualification, as the progress of our knowledge continues to throw
more light into the murky darkness of Buddhist chronology.

The authorship of the Iti-vuttaka, both prose and poetical portions, is attributed to the Blessed One, Buddha, and his teachings
are reported to have been heard and afterwards written down
by one of his disciples. The disciple keeps himself anonymous,
and contents himself with saying merely: 'This verily was said
by the Blessed One, said by the Sanctified One, so I have heard.'
There is nothing to disprove the authenticity of the stanzas in
the Iti-vuttaka as Buddha's own sayings; some scholars may be
inclined to hold, as some have already held about those in the
Jātakas and elsewhere, that the moral teachings in this work
may have been current in India long before Buddha's time, and
may have been adapted and changed by him to suit his own

purposes. But it seems doubtful to me that the prose portions of the Iti-vuttaka came originally from Buddha's mouth, although others may hold a different opinion. In many cases, as will be noted more particularly (see p. 9), the prose portions bear all the ear-marks of a short commentary on the succeeding verses; these prose portions our anonymous redactor may have written himself, or they may have been done previously by another and thus lay ready to his hand when the redactor undertook his compilation. At best their authorship seems highly uncertain.

Subject Matter. A glance at the table of contents which I have prefixed to the volume shows the Iti-vuttaka to be a collection of ethical teachings of Buddha, on a wide range of moral subjects. Passion, Anger, Pride, Lust, and other short-comings of body, word, and thought, are inveighed against or deprecated. Friendliness, Charity, Virtue, Modesty, and Truth are among the good qualities which the Master inculcates. Several characteristic Buddhist doctrines, the technical terms for which are hard to translate adequately, are dwelt upon; among them are Nirvāna, the Aggregates, the Substrata, Previous Existence, and Supreme Enlightenment.

It is to be noted that Buddha's rules and commands and dicta are seldom directed to mankind in general, but are usually addressed to his *bhikkhus,* his 'monks, mendicants, members of his order,' as the word may be translated. The *bhikkhunī,* or 'female devotee, nun,' is only once mentioned in the course of the work (§ 69). Sinners have the terrors of perdition preached to them to deter them from misdoing; to the virtuous there is promised Deliverance and escape from this imprisoning body, as a reward for their good deeds. Seldom is the didactic tone of the work broken by matters of a different tenor; yet, here and there, a changing note is heard. This point is well illustrated in the curious passage about the crossing of species in § 42, and in another way in § 107, by a portrayal of the attitude of the Buddhists toward the brahman householders, to whom they owed their sustenance. Occasional metaphors or similes add a pleasing touch to the style, as will be noted more particularly below.

Proper Names in the Text. Buddha is mentioned many times and under many titles. The word 'Buddha' itself is a title meaning the 'Enlightened One, the Wise One,' and it is to be noted that the great reformer's true name, Gotama, never occurs in the course of this book. Among his other appellatives are found the epithets of the 'Blessed One,' the 'Sanctified One,' the 'Consummate One,' the 'Great Sage,' the 'Master,' the 'Teacher,' and others. His cousin and arch-enemy, Devadatta, is once referred to (§ 89h). Māra, or Satan the tempter, is named no less than five times (§§ 58, 68, 82, 83, 93). I have noticed only a single geographical name, the reference being to 'Vulture-Peak,' a mountain in the Magadha country (§ 24).

The Uddānas. Scattered at varying intervals throughout the course of the text are found brief metrical résumés, in the Pāli language, of the particular sections that precede each. The word *uddāna* has the same spelling in Sanskrit as in Pāli, and means, literally, 'binding together, fastening,' and secondarily, 'table of contents, summary, résumé.' Although Monier-Williams in his Sanskrit Dictionary notes the fact that the native lexicographers assign this secondary meaning to the word in Sanskrit, there is no actual citation of its occurrence in any Sanskrit text. In Pāli, however, the meaning 'summary,' or 'résumé' is common, and the word *uddāna* is found in other books of the Buddhist canon, for example in the Sutta-Piṭaka. In the Iti-vuttaka there are eleven of these résumés. Eight of them sum up, or recapitulate very briefly, the ten sections of the work immediately preceding each; one résumé sums up seven preceding sections, another sums up thirteen sections, and still another refers to twenty-two sections immediately before it. This latter résumé, however, is in part a repetition of the one preceding, and we may note incidentally that this repeated portion shows wide variation in wording from the same matter in the previous résumé. The fact that the résumés in eight instances give a recapitulation of the series of ten sections preceding is not significant of anything especial; this choice of ten sections is, in my opinion, purely a mechanical arrangement and does not indicate that the ten in question have any particular interconnection. This opinion is plainly borne out by the fact that the second *uddāna* happens to fall between two sections (§§ 20 and 21) closely related in subject matter, style, and treatment.

The form of the *uddānas,* as already stated, is metrical, although the versification is but a sorry affair in spite of the efforts made to attain it. The native redactor's method of procedure was to take some salient or important word or words from each section, and to arrange in metrical form the various words thus obtained. In order to satisfy the requirements of the meter, he has been obliged to resort to various makeshifts and expedients. Sometimes a word is given in its stem form, and sometimes in the nominative case, according as the final syllable of the word in question is required by the meter to be light or heavy; sometimes, in order to fill in an extra syllable or two that may be exacted by the meter, a word is given in some case other than the nominative. For these latter instances see Uddāna 5. 4, 7, 8; 6. 3; 9. 4; 11. 4. Singulars instead of the plurals in the text passages are used, and vice versa. Worse than this, the redactor frequently not only does not give a word from the text at all, but even goes to the extent of substituting a word or expression of his own. This latter procedure may, and often does, meet the situation demanded by the meter, but, to me at least, seems to vitiate the value of these résumés. Another drawback, and again a serious one, to the value of the *uddānas,* is the fact that a certain word chosen to sum up, or recapitulate, a section, is a word which is neither salient nor important, but on the contrary, is quite subordinate in the section thus summarized. This again offers, in my opinion, a proof of the lack of value which the résumés have for any purpose whatsoever. Compare, for example, Uddāna 2. 2; 3. 1, 2; 4. 1, 2, 4; 5. 3; 7. 2; 9. 3; 10. 2, 3; 11. 2, 4. It is to be noted, furthermore, that all the *uddānas* refer back to the prose portions, and when, therefore, the prose and the poetical portions of a section are different in subject matter, as happens occasionally, the verse portion is not touched upon at all in the résumé.

As regards the meter in which the *uddānas* are written, it is found that ten are composed in the *śloka* meter, but a *śloka* of a highly irregular character, having, as it often does, verses with more than eight syllables. So irregular, in fact, are the verses of the *uddānas,* and so manifestly artificial is their character, that I have not included them in my metrical analysis of the work. As regards the sixth *uddāna,* the only one which is not written in the *śloka* meter, we are tempted to assume different authorship; this sixth résumé is written in a regular *triṣṭubh* meter, with four verses of eleven syllables each, and all the feet of each one of the four lines are normal. It is to be noted further that this résumé is the most accurate of the eleven in the book.

In general we may say of the résumés that they are merely jingles of little utility and less precision, abounding in errors of many kinds, loose in execution, and, in short, extremely ineffectual.

Connection between the Sections. Although, as said before, the Iti-vuttaka is a collection of short disquisitions on widely different moral subjects, there nevertheless does exist in many parts of the work an apparent sequence in the contents and subject matter of the different stanzas. The most common relationship between such interdependent stanzas is one of contrast—contrast between that which is good and that which is bad, between temperance and intemperance, between a moral man and an immoral man. Examples of such contrasting stanzas are found in §§ 20 and 21, 28 and 29, 32 and 33, 54 and 55, 56 and 57, 64 and 65, 70 and 71. A noticeable fact in these contrasts between good and bad, is that the evil attribute always has the first place, while the good attribute has the second. Other kinds of inter-sectional relationship besides this one of contrast, are to be found. At the opening of the book, the first six stanzas are all practically identical, save for the use in each of a different word for a different sin. Except for this single word, the six stanzas are absolutely alike. The series is summed up in a section of similar character (§ 7), which epitomizes the preceding six in the word *sabba,* ' the All.' Exactly the same series is again repeated without the least variation in §§ 9–13, but there the corresponding prose introductions are different from those in the group preceding. Another shorter group of stanzas similar to each other in content is found in §§ 52–56, where the first, third, and fifth stanzas of the group are identical, except for the varying cardinal words, like *vedanā*, 'feelings,' *esanā*, 'cravings,' and *āsavā*, 'taints.' In other parts of the work sundry less extensive parallel and similar phrases and expressions are to be noticed, but in these latter cases, the inter-stanza relationship is not so pronounced as in the examples just cited.

Repetition of Passages. Not only are a few sections couched in phraseology that is nearly identical, but downright repetitions as well are found. It is to be remarked that these repeated passages are not contiguous or even near to each other, but are widely separated. For example, 15 a–h = 105 a–h; 22 a–h = 60 a–h; 35 e–j = 36 e–j; 38 h–i = 46 c–d; 48 i–l = 91 e–h; 51 a–j = 76 g–n; 53 e–h = 72 e–h = 85 e–h; 68 a–b = 69 a–b; 86 e–f = 110 a–b; 93 w–b′ = 95 k–p. All these citations are taken from the verse portions. A few examples from the prose parts of the work might also be included, but they are passed over as being of minor importance. In my opinion, the fact that these repeated passages occur at such wide intervals in the composition strengthens the view already advanced, that the Iti-vuttaka is not a continuous work, but is rather a compilation, an arrangement of material previously composed, at some time not known to us.

Construction. It has already been stated that each of the 112 sections of the Iti-vuttaka consists roughly of two equal portions of prose and verse. For purposes of convenience we may examine these two parts separately, and we shall find this procedure of great advantage, as the treatment of each must necessarily be different.

Prose. In judging of the style of a literary composition, we must not merely examine and study the form, but we should also give appropriate attention to the subject matter, the question of the author's purpose, and the influence of contemporary and previous literary works. Thus, in estimating the Iti-vuttaka, we must remember that the purpose of the prose portions is to introduce and amplify, to explain and expound the moral stanzas which follow. As these stanzas contain practically no mythological, historical, biographical, or narrative passages, and as their prose introductions adhere in general very closely to the subject matter, we do not find in the prose divisions, for example, the charming folk-lore of the Jātakas, the vivid images of jewels, trees, mountain, and flowing river of the Jinālaṅkāra, the fascinating devil stories of the Saṁyutta Nikāya (cf. Warren, *Buddhism,* p. 426). Furthermore, the religious teachings of the Iti-vuttaka are not seasoned with the piquant, homely details and incidents of daily life, as are the doctrines of the Dīgha Nikāya. On the contrary there is in the present work a marked and close adherence to the main subject matter, so much so that one welcomes such a description as that of the sharks and demons in § 69 as a pungent example of Buddhist folk-lore. The prose style is, in general, bald, abrupt, inelegant. It is matter-of-fact and long-winded; it abounds in repetitions. The repetitions are both of phrase and formula, and it is of the latter that we shall speak first.

Formulas. At the opening of every prose portion of the Iti-vuttaka, with the exception of §§ 81–98, and 101–111, which will be discussed later, there is the formal sentence—'This verily was said by the Blessed One, said by the Sanctified One, so I have heard,' and at the close of each a second formula—'To this effect spake the Blessed One, and hereupon said the following.' This second formula refers to the poetical portion which immediately follows. At the end of the poetical portion there is adjoined a third formula—'Exactly to that effect was it spoken by the Blessed One, so I have heard.' These formulas indicate clearly the Buddhistic view, that not only the verse, but also the prose comes actually from Buddha's own lips. As indicated above, however, the prose portions were probably not spoken by Buddha at all, but are, it is likely, later than his time, and are a commentary on the Teacher's sayings in verse.

Dialogue Form. A conversational turn is given to the prose by the incessant repetition of the vocative *bhikkhave,* ' O monks.' The use of this word may be thought possibly to give an esoteric coloring to the teachings. In most of the sections, the dialogue form is further emphasized by direct questions, for example in the opening sentence of § 54: 'There are these three Cravings, O monks.' 'What three?' 'The Craving for Lust, the Craving for . . . ,' etc.

Repetition. Besides the repetition of a formula, there is also found, especially in the latter half of the work, a considerable, and sometimes rather tiresome, reiteration of phrases and sentences. This fact is of course no new thing in a Buddhist book, and the general view is that such repetitions were for pedagogic purposes. Without entering on the difficult problem as to how long Buddhistic doctrines were handed down by oral tradition, it is certain that oral tradition did at one time prevail, and that in the Iti-vuttaka, as in other canonical works, the frequent repetition was for mnemonic or didactic reasons.

Relation between the Prose and the Verse. The most casual perusal of the Iti-vuttaka confirms, it seems to me, the statement made above that the prose portions of the 112 sections are disguised commentaries on the metrical portions of these 112 sections. In § 18, for example, the verse says—'One that doth disturb the Order is tormented for an aeon in perdition.' The prose portion says on the same topic—'There is one thing, O monks, which, in coming into being, ariseth to the disadvantage and unhappiness of many people, to the detriment, disadvantage, and misery of many people, gods as well as men.' 'What is this one thing?' 'It is dissension in the Order. For in an Order that hath been divided, there are reciprocal quarrels as well as reciprocal abuse, reciprocal disagreement and desertion, and there (in such an Order) they are discontented and enjoy no contentment, and there is diversity of opinion (even) among those who are content.' Many similar examples might be adduced as illustrations of the point. Even more decisive evidence is at hand, it seems to me, in § 109. This section contains an allegorical

passage about the Flood of Passion, with an enumeration of the
dangers of the Flood. The prose takes up the different allegorical details, and proceeds to elucidate them as follows: '"Flood
of the river" is the designation of Thirst; "pleasant and delightful in aspect" is allegorically the designation of private dwellings;
"a pool below" is the designation of the five Bonds of sensual
life; "with waves" is the designation of the frenzy of anger;
"with whirlpools" is the designation of the five varieties of
Lust; "with crocodiles and demons" is the designation of womankind; "against the flood" is the designation of Separation;
"struggling with hands and feet" is the designation of the
exertion of one's strength; "the spectator standing on the shore"
is the designation of the Consummate One, the Sanctified One,
the Perfectly Enlightened One.' Occasionally when the stanza
is difficult of comprehension, or involved in impenetrable subtlety,
the writer of the introductory prose adroitly crawls out of the
difficulty and cleverly conceals his own miscomprehension of the
verses, either by giving the baldest, broadest possible outlines of
the verse, or by summing up the meaning in an ambiguous
word or phrase. The latter point is best illustrated by § 63,
which, in my judgment, is the most difficult section of the whole
book. A fuller treatment of this subject will be given in the
course of the translation, in the notes on the various sections.

Another possible confirmation of this view as to the prose
of the Iti-vuttaka, may be found in the more or less independent
subject matter included in it for the purpose of filling out and
amplifying the stanzas that follow. Although we hold to the
above opinion as to the prose, it is by no means our intention to
belittle its general value or its general interest. On the contrary
the prose, although not so interesting as the verse, contains much
that is of deep philosophical import, and its ethical dicta, although
perhaps somewhat lacking in rhetorical polish, are lofty and noble
in the extreme.

Poetry. Before discussing the style and substance of the
stanzas, it would be expedient to give here a full discussion of
their form, that is of the meters in which they are composed.

But owing to the length and somewhat technical character of this metrical analysis, it seems unnecessary to include such a discussion, of interest only to the specialist, within the confines of this more or less general introduction. The metrical analysis of the Iti-vuttaka will be found in the Journal of the American Oriental Society, New Haven, Conn., vol. 28, pp. 317-330. In that article I have classified the various types of meter found in the Iti-vuttaka, and have arranged statistical tables. I have also made a comparison with Vedic meters and likewise with those of Epic poetry in Sanskrit.

Style. Turning to the style of the stanzas in the book, we may appropriately devote a word of praise to their general simplicity. Hardly any trace is found of the artificial diction occasionally present in other Pāli works, for example, in the professedly rhetorical· Jinālaṅkāra of Buddharakkhita (edited and translated by James Gray, London, 1894), where we find (p. 10) the reversible line *namo tassa yato mahimato yassa tamo na,* which Gray renders: 'Honor to him (Buddha), inasmuch as to him, deserving of honor, no darkness is.' No such artificialities are found in the Iti-vuttaka; there is likewise a total lack of internal rhyme, and also of the so-called paragrammatic echoing rhymes. Occasional instances of paronomasia are to be found, for example in § 90, a passage of some interest, owing to the play on the word *agga,* ' chief, top,' a term repeated eleven times in the course of the stanzas.

Figures of Speech. Great assistance was obtained in making an examination of the rhetorical make-up of the Iti-vuttaka, from an opportune article by Mrs. Rhys Davids, entitled 'Similes in the Nikāyas,' in the Journal of the Pāli Text Society, London, 1906-7. The article consists of a painstaking list in Pāli of similes in the whole range of books composing the Sutta-piṭaka, and it offers evidence of the most diligent toil.

In general the use of figures of speech in the Iti-vuttaka, while not sparing, is hardly abundant, there being a round fifty in the work. Although a few rather striking similes and metaphors are found, they are as a rule not especially vivid. We

may conveniently divide the figures of speech into (*a*) those
drawn from the realm of nature; (*b*) those from animals and their
actions, and (*c*) those from man and his relations in daily life.

(*a*) Among the most common figures of speech are similes
based upon some natural phenomenon, the element of water play-
ing an important part. This prominence of similes drawn from
water is due to the frequent occurrence of the Buddhistic image
that the righteous man is he that crosses (*tarati*) beyond, or to
the other side (*pārā*) of the Flood (*ogha*) of Passion and Lust.
The latter word, *ogha,* occurs but once (§ 107) in the course of
the work, but the idea of crossing over it, *taranam,* to the other
shore, is quite frequent, as it occurs a dozen of times. Another
more common word for the same idea is *sammudha,* 'ocean,' in
the expression 'he crosseth the ocean . . . difficult to traverse'
(§ 69 c). The impulse of Passion or Desire is compared to a
river (*nadī*) of rapid current (*sota*), with many a treacherous
whirlpool (*āvaṭṭa*) to catch the helpless struggler (see § 109).
Different from this is the figure of the River of Subsistence
(*āhāra-netti*) in § 43. The drop of water (*uda-bindu,* § 88 l) and
the pool (*rahada,* § 92 i) are other forms of aqueous metaphors.

Almost as frequent as the water comparisons are the various
similes and metaphors based upon light. The sun and moon are
naturally foremost among the more concrete images, and each is
mentioned twice in the work (§§ 59 d, 88 a' and §§ 27, 74 i, respectively). In the first moon-passage, we find mention also of
the morning-star, *osadhi-tārakā.* Luminous terms in comparisons
are many; to the general word for light, *pabhā* (§§ 27, 104),
must be added *pajjotā,* 'brightness' (§ 104), *obhāsa,* 'radiance,'
āloka, 'splendor.' The monks must be 'torch-bearers' for the
laymen who are in darkness. To the same category of images
from the realm of light, belongs the passage on the 'funeral-
torch' (§ 91) which illumines the village dunghill. Contrasting
with these words, is the threefold occurrence of the idea of 'darkness' in §§ 14 f, 38 e, 47 h.

Two other nature-images of a different kind are the vivid description of the bursting of a rain-cloud, with its resultant inun-

dation (§ 75 o), and the eloquent stanzas in § 24 with their simile of the lofty mountain of Vulture Peak.

(b) Turning next to the animal similes, we find that animal imagery is rare. The lion, *sīha* (§ 112), the fish, *maccha* (§ 76), and the shark or crocodile, *gaha* (§§ 69, 109), alone are mentioned in comparisons; we might, however, include with them the *rakkhasas,* or 'demons' (§ 69) which inhabit the ocean. An animal likeness is perhaps also to be discerned in the epithet *siṅgi,* 'horned,' that is applied to a sinning monk in § 108.

(c) Much richer than the animal category, is the third class of similes and metaphors, namely, those derived from man and his relations in daily life. An interesting paragraph, probably to be taken allegorically, is found in § 74, where there occurs a description of children who are superior or equal or inferior to their parents. A prototype of Bunyan's hero, Christian, casting off his load, occurs in § 44, where the Sanctified monk is said to have 'laid his burden aside.' In § 68, we hear the words of an Oriental psalmist, as it were, in the scathing epithet applied to erring sinners who are called in biting phrase 'Bond of Māra, ye snare of Māra (*i. e.* the Devil).' A fine image occurs in §§ 28, 29, where the monks are exhorted to keep the 'doors' to their senses closely guarded. The 'door' is used again in personification in § 84 where the Great Sage and his faithful followers are said to disclose the 'door of Immortality (*dvāram amatassa*).'

Among other objects of every-day life which are used figuratively, may be mentioned the arrow (*sara*) that imparts to its quiver (*kalāpa*) the poison with which it is smeared (§ 76). Further the javelin (*salla*) is used symbolically of pain or suffering (§ 53). Various other comparisons, drawn this time from the vegetable realm, are of less importance; such for example is the figurative use of *mūla,* 'root' (§ 42 c), *tasa-sara,* 'of excellent bark,' *i. e.* the bamboo (§ 56), and *tala-pakka,* 'the ripe Tāl fruit, or Palmyra (§ 88 x). Finally we may refer to two epithets applied to the Master, Buddha, one where he is called the 'charioteer,' and the other, an interesting phrase found in § 100, where he calls himself 'the brahman . . . a healer, or physician, who is a " causer of pain," *sallakatta.*'

Synonyms and Titles of Buddha. Reference has already been made (p. 4) to the use in the Iti-vuttaka of many titles and appelatives given to Gotama. Although one would of course presuppose a use of such epithets in the course of the prose portions of the work, we would hardly expect to find them in the verses, which are professed to be the Master's own words to his disciples. He is spoken of impersonally in the verses as *Buddha,* 'the Enlightened One' (§§ 21 d, 35 h, 36 h, 52 b, 54 b, 56 b, 68 e, 90 c, 112 i, m) ; as *Tathāgata Buddha,* 'the Consummate, Enlightened One' (§§ 38 a, 39 a) ; as *Tathāgata* alone, 'the Consummate One' (§ 89 j, u) ; as *Sammāsambudha,* 'the Perfectly Enlightened One' (§§ 51 i, 73 m). Occasionally other adjectives are employed, such as, for example, *Bhagavan,* 'the Blessed One' (§§ 35 c, 36 c, 98 b), *Mahesi,* the 'Great Sage' (§§ 24 d, 26 b, 35 f, 36 f, 84 a), and also *Parisuttama,* 'the Excellent One' (§ 61 d). This inclusion of the word *Buddha* or other titles for Gotama within the stanzas themselves neither proves nor disproves his authorship of them.

Use of Internal Quotations. In further connection with this whole question of quotation, that is to say, of citation of formulas within the stanzas, which attest Buddha as the author, we may note the fact that in one stanza (§ 69 h) the Master's words are given direct, 'with the added words *iti brūmi,* 'so I say, so I declare,' within the stanza itself. This direct discourse is also found several times in the Dhammapada, compare, for example, verses 409–414 and many others. Redundant quotes of an indirect character, that is to say in the third person, are found in the following verses: *yathā vuttam mahesinā,* 'so was it said by the Great Sage' (§ 26 b), and *akkāsi parisuttamo,* 'the Excellent One hath proclaimed' (§ 61 d). In my opinion these lines were introduced into the stanzas by the compiler of the Iti-vuttaka, in order to fill the metrical requirements to give the stanzas the proper number of verses. That is, it seems probable that the compiler took from some earlier work, whether an oral or a writ-

ten one, it is not known, a certain number of verses; in order to
have of these verses the number requisite to make a complete
group, or stanza, he added in the stanza such superfluous state-
ments of Buddha's authorship. Additional confirmation of this
view is to be found, it seems to me, in the words *ti me sutam,*
'so I have heard,' introduced into verse h of § 89.

Stanzas not addressed to the Laity. Although the poetical portion of the Iti-vuttaka is far from being so didactic as the prose
that paraphrases it, nevertheless in the stanzas themselves the
didactic element is well marked. The appeal of this collection
of Buddha's teachings was not addressed to the laity in general,
for, as remarked above, they were directed to his *bhikkhus,* the
Brethren of the Buddhist Order. Although the term *bhikkhu,*
'monk,' does not occur in the stanzas with the same tiresome
frequency with which it is reiterated in the prose, yet the word
is found no less than thirty times within the verses of this book.
This frequent occurrence of the word 'monk' deserves some
emphasis, in order to point out forcibly that Buddha's teaching,
as set forth in the Iti-vuttaka, was distinctly not a world-teaching,
a wide, universal exhortation of mankind to higher ideals, but
was, on the contrary, confined to a comparatively narrow circle
of monastic followers.

Inter-canonical Quotation. The view has been more than once
advanced in this essay that the Iti-vuttaka is probably a compilation from various works of the Pāli canon; if this view be right,
the date of the compilation of the Iti-vuttaka must of course be
later than the composition of the other Buddhistic works from
which it is derived. Although this view may be substantiated in
several ways from internal evidence, it cannot, unfortunately, be
definitely proved until a complete concordance of all the canonical
works (some of which have not yet even been edited), has been
made. While preparing this translation, I made a beginning
of such a concordance, or cross-reference work, commencing with
the Jātakas, and had collected a large number of index slips, when
I learned that Professor R. O. Franke, of Königsberg, was
already at work upon a complete first-line index of the Pāli

canon, which is to be published in the Harvard Oriental Series. Accordingly I abandoned the task so as to avoid a duplication of the work. It is not possible, therefore, to settle the interesting question of inter-canonical quotation until Dr. Franke's valuable concordance is completed. A few such cross-references, however, may be made, to show the possibility of further developments in this line. The Iti-vuttaka, for instance, has four passages in common with the Dhammapada, a work which is itself a compilation, or anthology. Thus Iti-v., §§ 25 a–d, and 48 a–l, are identical with Dhp., vs. 176, 306–8. Not only are these four verses common to the two works, but many intangible likenesses in style, in expression, and in phrasing are to be observed. Several rather brief identical passages are to be found in the Samyutta Nikāya (edited by Feer, *PTS.*, London, 1884–1904), and these are noted by Windisch in the critical notes to his edition. Many long passages in the latter sections of the Iti-vuttaka, he observes, are repeated, *verbatim*, in the Anguttara Nikāya. This coincidence, when taken together with the different character generally of the latter part of the Iti-vuttaka, and also in connection with the fact that so many of the latter sections are not to be found in the Chinese translation of the work by Yuan Chwāng (Hüan Tsang) (see Watanabe, *Chinese Collection of Iti-vuttakas,* in *JPTS.*, London, 1907, pp. 44–49), seems, in my opinion, to show that many of the latter sections of this book are of later introduction as compared with the former portions.

Grammar. In the course of this translation there are given in the notes a number of interesting grammatical points presented by the language of the Iti-vuttaka, both in respect to inflection and syntax. Although a discussion of such matters would naturally be out of place here, we may briefly outline a few of the more important questions. In inflection there occur several archaic plurals, which we may term Vedic plurals, and which are occasionally found elsewhere in Pāli. Thus *luddhāse, dutthāse, mulhāse, kuddhāse, makkhāse, mattāse* in the first six sections, in place of the more usual forms *luddhā, dutthā, mulhā,* etc. One instance of the use of a dative case as an infinitive is worth noting (see § 86, note 1). There are two examples of the exceedingly rare conditional mood, *agamissa* (§ 42. 7), and *abhavissa* (§ 43. 3). In syntax we may note the very common use of the gerund and gerundive, particularly of the former. The gerund ending *-tvāna*, corresponding to the Vedic *-tvānam* occurs nine times. The use of the aorist as an indefinite past tense is very common, occurring on every page of the book. The syntax of the stanzas is usually quite simple, but occasional inversions and omissions of verbs are found, and these instances will be found treated in the notes. The style is somewhat marred by the frequent use of the indefinite relative clause, and this slight stylistic blemish, or mannerism, is but too manifest, I fear, in the translation.

Vocabulary. The choice of words in the Iti-vuttaka is naturally dependent on the subject matter, and is to be expected that the words should be largely religious terms. The work is rich in categorical moral terms, with their opposites, such as Friendliness, Charity, Virtue, Lust, Hate, Sloth, and many others. In rendering these words into English a translator is beset with a task of some difficulty. The various European translators of Buddhistic works show great lack of accord in their ways of translating these and other cardinal words. I have naturally felt some hesitation in deviating from such great scholars as have helped to open up the vast field of Buddhist history and religion, but it is absolutely impossible to keep in harmony with all, so that an eclectic attitude has been adopted. Where, however, there is general accord among European translators—such as, for example, in the translation of the Pāli terms *upādi, khanda, samkhāra, samkhata,* by 'Substrata,' 'Attribute,' 'Aggregate,' 'Compound'—I have not differed from them save for the weightiest reasons.

Besides this matter there are other obstacles before a translator. Even where the meaning of a certain Pāli word is clear, and when only a single English equivalent exists, this English word unfortunately has sometimes one or more connotations which do not belong to the Pāli term at all. Such, for example,

3

is the word *vimutti*, rendered 'Emancipation,' for here the English, as I think, has a religious implication foreign to the Pāli. To avoid having the reader in this way read too much into the Pāli sentences, owing to his having taken the English with too full an extension perhaps, I have adopted, where necessary, the plan of capitalizing the English words, thus—Sin, Delusion, Faith, and similar terms. The reader will, therefore, be on his guard against taking such words in their full English meaning with all nuances and connotations. For the convenience of the reader a list of the more important Pāli terms, with my English renderings of them, is included in the index.

Other Difficulties of Translation. The question of Pāli etymology is largely based on comparison with analogous forms in Sanskrit. A blind adherence to Sanskrit as an aid to solving questions of etymology in Pāli is not to be indulged in, for without doubt the Pāli language, although it has the greatest similarity with the Sanskrit in grammar and vocabulary, has cut out for itself, in many respects, entirely new linguistic paths. The rise of Buddhism, and also of the Jaina sect, taken together with the ever-increasing use of Pāli as a means of literary expression, was not without influence on the Sanskrit.

Unfortunately, however, there are times when etymology is both doubtful and perplexing. In this particular respect it must be said that the Pāli dictionary of Childers (London, 1875) is often inadequate and faulty, but we could not expect it to be otherwise of such a pioneer work. To say that this dictionary abounds in omissions, errors, mistakes, and confusions, or to say that its list of words is from a very limited portion of Pāli literature, is merely to say that it is the first and only occidental dictionary of the Pāli language. Considering the paucity of published texts in Childers' day, the retarded state of philological information at the time, and the general lack of facilities for such a work, we must look on his achievement as little short of marvelous. But from the nature of the case, the book is unreliable in many respects. Turning to the grammars of Pāli which we now have, we find much left to be desired. For etymological purposes Franke's *Pāli und Sanskrit* (Strassburg, 1902) is of great use. The same may be said of the *Grammaire Pâlie* of Henry (Paris, 1904), though it errs in many ways both in treatment and content. A comprehensive grammar of Pāli, similar to Whitney's *Sanskrit Grammar*, would fill a long-felt need, as would also a biographical and mythological Buddhist encyclopedia. In etymology, therefore, as in other matters, rigorous testing must be done at every step, and the suggestions that are here given in the notes as to new solutions are presented with the caution proper in the present state of Pāli linguistics. The meaning of such a word as *nipaka*, ' prudent,' for example, is fairly certain, but its etymology is far from clear; *vice versa* there are one or two instances of words whose etymology is obvious, but whose precise significance it is almost hopeless to determine.

It seems desirable in a work of this character to try to render a word always by a constant, unchanging English word. But although this process may be advisable as a rule, it is by no means always feasible in practice. As Paul Cauer, in his admirable little work, *Die Kunst des Übersetzens,* Berlin, 1894, p. 48, indicates from the classical standpoint, a qualifying adjective, a varying context, a change in locution, frequently necessitates a different rendering for the same word of the text. In this present translation it has sometimes been necessary to follow this procedure; a noun and a verb, or a noun and an adjective, for instance, which may come from the same Pāli root, have had occasionally to be translated by two words from different roots in English.

It is hoped, furthermore, that the plentiful citation of the obscurer or less common Pāli words within parentheses will enable the reader to use this translation for comparative purposes by the side of other translations from Pāli texts. It has been thought best to give throughout a fairly literal rendering. The conciseness of the Pāli makes the unavoidable amplitude of the English seem somewhat rigid and verbose in comparison. It is hoped that my strict adherence to the original will not

be found too close; for when it has become a question of prefer-
ence between an elegant rendering and one awkward but more
accurate, I have purposely always chosen the latter. It was
found impossible to make a metrical translation of the stanzas
which should be at all faithful or close to the original. As an
aid to the appreciation of the spirit, or tone, of the book, I have
made use of the archaic English ending *-eth* in the verbal forms
throughout.

SAYINGS OF BUDDHA

HAIL TO THAT BLESSED ONE, THAT SANCTIFIED ONE, SUPREME BUDDHA

§ 1. This verily was said by the Blessed One, said by the Sanctified One, so I have heard.

'One of the Laws, O monks, ye do forsake. I am your surety, in that I have entered the path from which there is no return.'[1] 'Which one of the Laws?' 'Ye forsake, O monks,[2] the law against Desire (*lobha-*). I am your surety in that I have entered the path from which there is no return.'

To this effect spake the Blessed One, and hereupon said the following:

'Through their proper knowledge
Creatures of Discernment[3] forsake that Desire
Through which lustful creatures[4]
Go to misfortune.
When they have forsaken it
They never return to this world.'

Exactly to that effect was it spoken by the Blessed One, so I have heard.

§ 2. This verily was said by the Blessed One, said by the Sanctified One, so I have heard.

---

[1] *anāgāmitā-;* lit. 'the quality of being one who doth not return,' referring to the third of the four well-known *maggas,* or Paths.

[2] *bhikkhu-;* this word has been variously translated as 'priest, mendicant, mendicant-priest.' Although it does have an element of all these meanings, none of them is entirely satisfactory. Rhys Davids suggests 'member of the order' as a rendering, but, as he himself says, this translation of the word is too cumbrous to be practicable.

[3] *vi-passin-;* lit. 'seeing clearly, seeing thoroughly.' Compare the passage on the 'Spiritual Eyes,' § 61, and the word *cakkhumā,* §§ 45, 47, 104, 109.

[4] *luddhāse;* this lengthened plural form is comparable to the Vedic plural.

'One of the Laws, O monks, ye do forsake. I am your surety, in that I have entered the path from which there is no return.' 'Which one of the Laws?' 'Ye forsake, O monks, the Law against Hate (*dosa-*). I am your surety in that I have entered the path from which there is no return.'

To this effect spake the Blessed One, and hereupon said the following:

'Through their proper knowledge
Creatures of Discernment forsake that Hate
Through which hating creatures
Go to misfortune.
When they have forsaken it
They never return to. this world.'

Exactly to that effect was it spoken by the Blessed One, so I have heard.

§ 3. This verily was said by the Blessed One, said by the Sanctified One, so I have heard.

'One of the Laws, O monks, ye do forsake. I am your surety, in that I have entered the path from which there is no return.' 'Which one of the Laws?' 'Ye forsake, O monks, the Law against Delusion (*moha-*). I am your surety in that I have entered the path from which there is no return.'

To this effect spake the Blessed One, and hereupon said the following:

'Through their proper knowledge
Creatures of Discernment forsake that Delusion
Through which deluded creatures
Go to misfortune.
When they have forsaken it
They never return to this world.'

Exactly to that effect was it spoken by the Blessed One, so I have heard.

§ 4. This verily was said by the Blessed One, said by the Sanctified One, so I have heard.

'One of the Laws, O monks, ye do forsake. I am your surety, in that I have entered the path from which there is no return.' 'Which one of the Laws?' 'Ye forsake, O monks, the Law against Anger (*khoda-*). I am your surety in that I have entered the path from which there is no return.'

To this effect spake the Blessed One, and hereupon said the following:

> 'Through their proper knowledge
> Creatures of Discernment forsake that Anger
> Through which angry creatures
> Go to misfortune.
> When they have forsaken it
> They never return to this world.'

Exactly to that effect was it spoken by the Blessed One, so I have heard.

§ 5. This verily was said by the Blessed One, said by the Sanctified One, so I have heard.

'One of the Laws, O monks, ye do forsake. I am your surety, in that I have entered the path from which there is no return.' 'Which one of the Laws?' 'Ye forsake, O monks, the Law against Hypocrisy (*makkha-*). I am your surety in that I have entered the path from which there is no return.'

To this effect spake the Blessed One, and hereupon said the following:

> 'Through their proper knowledge
> Creatures of Discernment forsake that Hypocrisy
> Through which hypocritical creatures
> Go to misfortune.
> When they have forsaken it
> They never return to this world.'

Exactly to that effect was it spoken by the Blessed One, so I have heard.

§ 6. This verily was said by the Blessed One, said by the Sanctified One, so I have heard.

'One of the Laws, O monks, ye do forsake. I am your surety, in that I have entered the path from which there is no return.' 'Which one of the Laws?' 'Ye forsake, O monks, the Law against Pride (*māna-*). I am your surety in that I have entered the path from which there is no return.'

To this effect spake the Blessed One, and hereupon said the following:

> 'Through their proper knowledge
> Creatures of Discernment forsake that Pride
> Through which proud creatures
> Go to misfortune.
> When they have forsaken it
> They never return to this world.'

Exactly to that effect was it spoken by the Blessed One, so I have heard.

§ 7. This verily was said by the Blessed One, said by the Sanctified One, so I have heard.

'He, O monks, that doth not understand and comprehend the All (*sabba-*), and whose thought about it is neither one of renunciation nor abandonment, cannot attain destruction of Misery. But he that doth understand and comprehend the All, and whose thought about it is one of renunciation and abandonment, can attain destruction of Misery.'

To this effect spake the Blessed One, and hereupon said the following:

> 'Whoso doth wholly know the All,
> And rejoiceth not in all things—
> He, by his knowledge of the All,
> Hath passed beyond all Misery.'

Exactly to that effect was it spoken by the Blessed One, so I have heard.

§ 8. This verily was said by the Blessed One, said by the Sanctified One, so I have heard.

'He, O monks, that doth not understand and comprehend Pride, and whose thought about it is neither one of renunciation nor abandonment, cannot attain destruction of Misery. But he that doth understand and comprehend Pride, and whose thought about it is one of renunciation and abandonment, can attain destruction of Misery.'

To this effect spake the Blessed One, and hereupon said the following:

> ' This human kind[1] (that is) possessed of Pride,
> With shackles of Pride, and delighted by Existence,
> (And that) doth not comprehend Pride—
> They shall attain[2] rebirth.

> And those who, having forsaken Pride,
> Are freed from its destruction—
> They have overcome its shackles,
> And have passed beyond all Misery.'

Exactly to that effect was it spoken by the Blessed One, so I have heard.

§ 9. This verily was said by the Blessed One, said by the Sanctified One, so I have heard.

' He, O monks, that doth not understand and comprehend Desire, and whose thought about it is neither one of renunciation nor abandonment, cannot attain destruction of Misery. But he that doth understand and comprehend Desire, and whose thought about it is one of renunciation and abandonment, can attain destruction of Misery.'

To this effect spake the Blessed One, and hereupon said the following:

> ' Through their proper knowledge
> Creatures of Discernment forsake that Desire
> Through which lustful creatures
> Go to misfortune.
> When they have forsaken it
> They never return to this world.'

---

[1] pajā-, Skt. prajā-. The first two lines of this stanza are in the singular; the second two are in the plural. The logical subject throughout is pajā-.

[2] āgantāro; a periphrastic fut. See Whitney, Sanskrit Grammar, §§ 942–947.

Exactly to that effect was it spoken by the Blessed One, so I have heard.

§ 10. This verily was said by the Blessed One, said by the Sanctified One, so I have heard.

'He, O monks, that doth not understand and comprehend Hate, and whose thought about it is neither one of renunciation nor abandonment, cannot attain destruction of Misery. But he that doth understand and comprehend Hate, and whose thought about it is one of renunciation and abandonment, can attain destruction of Misery.'

To this effect spake the Blessed One, and hereupon said the following:

'Through their proper knowledge
Creatures of Discernment forsake that Hate
Through which hating creatures
Go to misfortune.
When they have forsaken it
They never return to this world.'

Exactly to that effect was it spoken by the Blessed One, so I have heard.

[End of the] First Chapter about the Surety

Résumé 1

Passion (§ 1)[1]; Hate (§ 2)[2]; then Delusion (§ 3)[3];
Anger (§ 4); Hypocrisy (§ 5); Pride (§ 6); the All (§ 7);
After Pride (§ 8); the two about Passion (§ 9)[1]; and Hate (§ 10);
These are revealed, they say, as the first chapter.

§ 11. This verily was said by the Blessed One, said by the Sanctified One, so I have heard.

---

[1] Observe the use of *rāga-*, 'passion' to gloss *lobha-*, 'desire,' of the text.

[2] This and the previous word are in a dvandva compound in the plural number.

[3] This word is put in the nom. case; the others, with the exception noted above, are in the stem form.

'He, O monks, that doth not understand and comprehend Delusion, and whose thought about it is neither one of renunciation nor abandonment, cannot attain destruction of Misery. But he that doth understand and comprehend Delusion, and whose thought about it is one of renunciation and abandonment, can attain destruction of Misery.'

To this effect spake the Blessed One, and hereupon said the following:

> 'Through their proper knowledge
> Creatures of Discernment forsake that Delusion
> Through which deluded creatures
> Go to misfortune.
> When they have forsaken it
> They never return to this world.'

Exactly to that effect was it spoken by the Blessed One, so I have heard.

§ 12. This verily was said by the Blessed One, said by the Sanctified One, so I have heard.

'He, O monks, that doth not understand and comprehend Anger, and whose thought about it is neither one of renunciation nor abandonment, cannot attain destruction of Misery. But he that doth understand and comprehend Anger, and whose thought about it is one of renunciation and abandonment, can attain destruction of Misery.'

To this effect spake the Blessed One, and hereupon said the following:

> 'Through their proper knowledge
> Creatures of Discernment forsake that Anger
> Through which angry creatures
> Go to misfortune.
> When they have forsaken it
> They never return to this world.'

Exactly to that effect was it spoken by the Blessed One, so I have heard.

§ 13. This verily was said by the Blessed One, said by the Sanctified One, so I have heard.

'He, O monks, that doth not understand and comprehend Hypocrisy, and whose thought about it is neither one of renunciation nor abandonment, cannot attain destruction of Misery. But he that doth understand and comprehend Hypocrisy, and whose thought about it is one of renunciation and abandonment, can attain destruction of Misery.'

To this effect spake the Blessed One, and hereupon said the following:

> 'Through their proper knowledge
> Creatures of Discernment forsake that Hypocrisy
> Through which hypocritical creatures
> Go to misfortune.
> When they have forsaken it
> They never return to this world.'

Exactly to that effect was it spoken by the Blessed One, so I have heard.

§ 14. This verily was said by the Blessed One, said by the Sanctified One, so I have heard.

'I see no other single impediment, O monks, by which man-kind[1] is so impeded, and caused for a long time to undergo rebirth and transmigration, as by the impediment of Ignorance. For by the impediment of Ignorance, O monks, mankind is impeded and for a long time is caused to undergo rebirth and transmigration.'

To this effect spake the Blessed One, and hereupon said the following:

> 'There is no other single thing
> By which mankind is so impeded
> And long undergoeth rebirth,
> As by the impediment of Delusion.[2]

---

[1] *pajā-;* here with the plural verb. See page 25, note 1.
[2] Lit. 'when obstructed by delusion.'

> Those who, forsaking Delusion,
> Have rent the Attribute[1] of Darkness,
> Do not undergo rebirth again,
> (Since) no cause for it is found in them.'

Exactly to that effect was it spoken by the Blessed One, so I have heard.

§ 15. This verily was said by the Blessed One, said by the Sanctified One, so I have heard.

' I see no other single fetter, O monks, by which creatures are so impeded, and caused for a long time to undergo rebirth and transmigration, as by the fetter of Thirst.[2] For by the fetter of Thirst, O monks, creatures are fettered, and for a long time are caused to undergo rebirth and transmigration.'

To this effect spake the Blessed One, and hereupon said the following:

> ' With Thirst as second a man undergoeth
> The long journey of transmigration (saṃsāra-)
> He doth not escape the rounds of existence
> Similar and dissimilar (to the present one).
>
> When he thus findeth that transgression (adīnava-)
> Is the source of the Misery of Thirst,
> The thoughtful monk is freed from Thirst and attachment
> And may lead a holy life.' [3]

Exactly to that effect was it spoken by the Blessed One, so I have heard.

§ 16. This verily was said by the Blessed One, said by the Sanctified One, so I have heard.

' For a novitiate-monk (sekkha-)[4] who hath not yet attained

---

[1] For a discussion of this important word khandha-, see Childers, Pāli Dictionary, s. v.

[2] tanhā-; many renderings have been attempted for this word, but I have thought best to give throughout its literal translation 'thirst.'

[3] paribbaje, opt., Skt. pari-vraj-, 'to wander about (as a mendicant).'

[4] sekkha- cf. Skt. śaikhsa-. There are seven stages of study, or meditation, leading up to the state of asekkha-, a syn. of Arahatship, 'Sanctification.' Compare Buddhaghosa's gloss on Dhp. verse 45. Fausböll renders 'discipulus.'

Supreme Security,[1] but who is striving for it, and who liveth
with the idea that what is internal (*ajjhattika-*) is a qualification (*anga-*), I see no other single qualification, O monks, so
exceeding helpful as profound attention (*manasikāra-*). A
(novitiate-)monk, then, O monks, who hath profound attention,
abandoneth impropriety and acquireth propriety.

To this effect spake the Blessed One, and hereupon said the
following:

'Attention that is profound
Is a law for the novitiate-monk;
There is no other law so exceeding helpful
For the attainment of the Summum Bonum (*uttama-attha-*).
By devoting himself profoundly, a monk
May attain destruction of Misery.'

Exactly to that effect was it spoken by the Blessed One, so I
have heard.

§ 17. This verily was said by the Blessed One, said by the
Sanctified One, so I have heard.

'For a novitiate-monk who hath not yet attained supreme Security, but who is striving for it, and who liveth with the idea
that what is external (*bāhira-*) is a qualification, I see no other
single qualification, O monks, so exceeding helpful as the quality
of having goodness (*kalyāna-*) as a friend. A (novitiate-)
monk, then, O monks, who hath goodness as his friend, re-
nounceth that which is evil, and obtaineth that which is good.'

To this effect spake the Blessed One, and hereupon said the
following:

'The monk that hath goodness as friend,
Who is obedient and respectful,
Doing the behest (*vacana-*) of his friends,

---

[1] *yogakkhema-;* lit. 'yoke of security,' although it may be dvandva compound. In Skt. the two members of this comp. are frequently in collocation,
viz., *yoga-ksema-*, and *ksema-yoga-*, denoting ' secure possession of what is
acquired.' See Monier Williams, *Skt. Dict.*, s. v.

> Mindful and thoughtful,
> May attain in due course
> The destruction of all the Fetters.'

Exactly to that effect was it spoken by the Blessed One, so I have heard.

§ 18. This verily was said by the Blessed One, said by the Sanctified One, so I have heard.

'There is one thing in the world, O monks, which, in coming into existence, existeth to the disadvantage and unhappiness of many people, to the detriment, disadvantage, and misery of many people, gods as well as men.' 'What is this one thing?' ' (It is) dissension in the Order. For in an Order that hath been divided, there are reciprocal (*aññamaññaṃ*) quarrels as well as reciprocal abuse, reciprocal disagreement and desertion, and there (*i. e.* in such an Order) they are discontented and enjoy no contentment, and there is diversity[1] of opinion (even) among those who are content.'

To this effect spake the Blessed One, and hereupon said the following:

> ' A disturber of the Order stayeth for an aeon
> In punishment and perdition;
> For he that delighteth in society (*vagga-*)
> And abideth not in the Law, falleth from Security[2];
> Having (also) broken up a concordant Order
> He burneth (lit. is cooked) for an aeon in perdition.'

Exactly to that effect was it spoken by the Blessed One, so I have heard.

§ 19. This verily was said by the Blessed One, said by the Sanctified One, so I have heard.

'There is one thing in the world, O monks, which, in coming into existence, existeth to the disadvantage, and unhappiness of many people, to the detriment, disadvantage and misery of many

---

[1] *aññathatta-*, anal. to Skt. *anyathā-atman-;* lit. 'variousmindedness.'
[2] See page 30, note 1.

people, gods as well as men.' ' What is this one thing?' ' (It
is) concord in the Order. For in a concordant Order, O
monks, there are neither reciprocal quarrels nor reciprocal abuse,
nor is there reciprocal disagreement and desertion, and there (*i. e.*
in such an Order) they are contented and enjoy contentment,
and among those who are contented there is further[1] (contentment).'

To this effect spake the Blessed One, and hereupon said the
following:

' Happy is the concord of the Order,
And the kindliness of those in concord,
For he that is delighted by concord,
And who abideth in the Law,
Falleth not from Security.
Having also made the Order concordant
He rejoiceth for an aeon in heaven.'

Exactly to that effect was it spoken by the Blessed One, so I
have heard.

§ 20. This verily was said by the Blessed One, said by the
Sanctified One, so I have heard.

' Here (in this world), O monks, comprehending thought by
means of thought, I thus recognize a certain individual as having
evil thought (*cetas-*), and this individual at this moment, having
completed his (allotted) time, just as is handed down by tradition,[2] has been cast into hell.' ' Why is this?' ' Because, O
monks, his thought is evil. For (*kho pana*) in this wise, certain
creatures on account of the corruption of their thoughts, after
the dissolution of the body after death, go to punishment, misfortune, torture, and perdition.'

---

[1] For Pāli *bhīyo*, Skt. *bhūyas*, see Franke, *Pāli und Sanskrit*, § 226, and
Henry, *Grammaire Pâlie*, § 23.

[2] *yathā bhatam;* I take *bhatam* as a pass. ppl. of root *bhr-*, ' to bear.' The
objection to this procedure is that the interpretation in question involves
giving a very uncommon meaning to the root *bhr-*. A tempting and easy
emendation of the text would be to read *yathābhūtam*, ' rightly, truly,' but
I prefer to force the meaning of *bhr-*.

To this effect spake the Blessed One; and hereupon said the following:

> ' Knowing a certain individual here
> As having evil thought,
> Buddha expounded this matter[1]
> In the presence of his monks.

> And at this moment,
> This individual, having completed his (allotted) time,[2]
> Shall attain perdition,
> Since his thought is evil.

> In just such wise will such a one
> Hereafter fare as is his due.
> It is because of their corrupt thoughts
> That creatures go to Misery.'

Exactly to that effect was it spoken by the Blessed One, so I have heard.

Résumé 2

Delusion (§ 11); Anger (§ 12); then Hypocrisy (§ 13);
Delusion (§ 14); Lust (§ 15)[3]; two about a novitiate-monk (§ 16 and § 17)[4];
Dissension (§ 18); Joy (§ 19)[5]; and an individual (§ 20).
This, they say, is called the second chapter.

[End of] the second chapter

[1] Observe the superfluous mention of Buddha's own name.

[2] The line in C, D, E, M, S reads *kālam kayirātha puggalo.* Its metrical scheme is — — ‿⌣ — | ‿ — ‿⌣, involving synizesis. The MSS. P and Pa read the second word *kariyā,* which I follow, first because as an opt. act. 3d sing., it corresponds phonetically with Skt. *kuryāt,* while *kayirātha,* if a 3d sing. as is required by the context, would have to be middle voice, and so extremely difficult of explanation; secondly because of the meter, which would now be — — ‿⌣ | — — ‿ —, avoiding synizesis.

[3] *kāma-* is used instead of *tanha-* of the text.

[4] *sekkha-,* 'novitiate-monk,' is not the important word of §§ 16, 17, but *manasikāra-,* 'perfect attention' and *kalyānamittatā-,* 'having goodness as a friend,' respectively.

[5] *moda-,* 'joy,' is not the text word, but *samghassa sāmaggī,* 'unity in the Order.'

§ 21. This verily was said by the Blessed One, said by the Sanctified One, so I have heard.

'Here (in this world), O monks, comprehending thought by means of thought, I thus recognize a certain individual as having tranquil thought, and this individual at this moment, having completed his (allotted) time, just as is handed down by tradition, hath been assigned (lit. cast into) heaven.' 'Why is this?' 'Because, O monks, his thought is tranquil. For in this wise, certain creatures on account of the tranquillity of their thoughts, after the dissolution of the body after death, go to prosperity and heaven.'

To this effect spake the Blessed One, and hereupon said the following:

'Knowing a certain individual here
As having tranquil thought,
Buddha expounded this matter
In the presence of his monks.

For at this moment,
This individual, having completed his (allotted) time,
Shall attain prosperity,
Since his thought is tranquil.

In just such wise will such a one
Hereafter fare as is his due.
It is because of their tranquil thoughts
That creatures go to prosperity.'

Exactly to that effect was it spoken by the Blessed One, so I have heard.

§ 22. This verily was said by the Blessed One, said by the Sanctified One, so I have heard.[1]

'Be not afraid of virtues (*puñña-*), O monks; this (*i. e.* the word *puñña-*, "virtuous") is the designation of what is happy, desirable, lovely, pleasing, and charming. Now I, forsooth, O

---

[1] The prose portion of this section has been translated by A. J. Edmunds, *Buddhist and Christian Gospels*, Tokyo, 1905, p. 142.

monks, have long recognized the long-desired, happy, lovely, pleasing, and charming reward respectively enjoyed[1] for virtuous deeds done.   Having devoted myself seven[2] years to the thought of Friendship, I did not return to this world for seven *samvat* aeons and (seven) Revolution aeons[3]; verily, O monks, at the end of a *samvat* aeon, I go unto the Radiant Ones[4]; at the end of a Revolution aeon, I reach the empty palace of Brahma.   There, verily, O monks, I become Brahma, the great Brahma,[5] surpassing, unsurpassed, comprehending the purpose of others,[6] and all-powerful.[7]

'Now I, forsooth, O monks, became Sakka, ruler of the gods, thirty-six times; many hundreds of times was I king, Universal Monarch (*cakka-vatti*), lawful king, victorious in the four quarters, maintaining the security of my dominions, possessed of the seven jewels.   Now what was the doctrine of that region and kingdom? This is what I thought of it, O monks: "Of what deed of mine is this the fruit? Of what deed is it the result, whereby I now have become of such great prosperity and such great might? Truly it is the fruit of three deeds of mine, it is the result of three deeds of mine, whereby I am at this time of such great prosperity and of such great might, namely, (the three deeds of) Charity (*dāna-*), of Self-command (*dama-*), and of Self-control (*saññama-*)."'

---

[1] *praty-anu-bhū-* is the Skt. analogy, lit. 'to enjoy one by one, severally.'

[2] Observe that the seven years are in a prior existence.

[3] A favorite Buddhist phraseology for very long periods of time.   See § 99.

[4] A class of 64 demigods.   See Apte and Monier Williams, s. v. *ābhasa-*.

[5] Buddha and Mahā Brahmā are usually quite distinct and separate personages.   Compare Warren, *Buddhism in Translations*, pp. 39, 47, 72, 77, 310.

[6] *aññadatthudasa-;* I would analyze this compound as *anya(d)-artha-dṛś*. The neuter form *anyad* occurs at the beginning of a compound in Skt.   For the *u* in *atthu* instead of *a*, cf. Franke, *Pāli und Sanskrit*, p. 103.   The collocation of *artha* and *dṛś-* is not unusual, being found, for example, in the Skt. comp. *arthadarśanam*, 'perception of objects.'   Consult Böhtlingk and Roth, *Sanskrit Wörterbuch*, under *anyad*.   The word occurs again in § 112.

[7] *vasavattī;* Childers translates this word 'bringing into subjection,' while Böhtlingk and Roth translate 'untertan, gehorsam.'   The word occurs again in the active sense in § 112, where I have likewise rendered it 'all-powerful,' and is found in the passive meaning in § 95.

To this effect spake the Blessed One, and hereupon said the following:

'One should learn virtue which is of extensive goal,
   And (which hath) the faculty[1] of Happiness;
   And one should devote oneself to Charity,
   To tranquil behavior (*samacariya-*) and to thoughts of Friendship.

Having devoted himself to these three virtues,
Which provide reason for happiness,
A wise man gaineth the world of happiness—
A world all free from distress.'

Exactly to that effect was it spoken by the Blessed One, so I have heard.

§ 23. This verily was said by the Blessed One, said by the Sanctified One, so I have heard.

' A single law, O monks, when practised and given force to[2] causeth the attainment[3] of both welfares, (namely) the present welfare and the future welfare.' 'What is this single law?' 'Zeal (*appamāda-*)[4] in good works. Just this law, O monks, when practised and given force to, causeth the attainment of both welfares, namely, the present and the future welfare.'

To this effect spake the Blessed One, and hereupon said the following:

' The wise praise zeal in virtuous deeds.
   A wise man who is zealous,
   Attaineth both welfares;

---

[1] Compare § 60, and see the note on *indriya,* 'faculty.'

[2] *bahulīkata-;* lit. 'made large, abundant.' Compare with Skt. *bahula-,* 'thick, abundant,' and *kṛta-,* 'made.' For the *ī* before *kṛ-,* cf. Whitney, *Sanskrit Grammar,* § 1093.

[3] *samadhigayha;* this compound is not in Childers, and no analogy exists in Skt. I take *gayha* as gerund of root *grabh-,* with the preps. *sam-adhi.* These two preps. imply motion towards, cf. Skt. *sam-adhi-gam-,* 'to go toward, approach.'

[4] Compare Skt. *a-pramāda-,* 'not-inattentive, not-careless, not-neglectful.'

The welfare which is in this seen world,
And the welfare in the future (world).
A man that is steadfast
In his grasp upon them
Is called wise.'

Exactly to that effect was it spoken by the Blessed One, so I have heard.

§ 24. This verily was said by the Blessed One, said by the Sanctified One, so I have heard.

'Of any individual who undergoeth transmigration, and who is reborn for an aeon (of time), there would be thus a great skeleton of bones, a mass of bones, a heap of bones, just like this huge mountain; if there should be made a gathering of them, the collection could not disappear.'

To this effect spake the Blessed One, and hereupon said the following:

'The heap of bones of every individual
For every deed, would be a pile
Like unto a mountain.
Thus the Great Sage hath said.[1]

And this mass is said to be
A mighty mountain
Higher than "Vulture-Peak"[2]
In Giribbaja of the Māgadhas.

And likewise through proper wisdom
One may see the Noble Truths:
Misery, its origin and its termination,
The holy Eightfold Path
That leadeth to the stilling[3] of Misery.

---

[1] Observe the superfluous mention of Buddha's name, as in § 20.

[2] A mountain near Rajagaha. Compare Lanman, *Sanskrit Reader*, p. 27, § V, line 1.

[3] *upasama-*, Skt. *upa-śam-*. See §§ 90 f, 87 e, 110 l, 103 p.

This individual being reborn seven times at most
Through the destruction of the Fetters,
Becometh a maker of the end of Misery.'

Exactly to that effect was it spoken by the Blessed One, so I have heard.

§ 25. This verily was said by the Blessed One, said by the Sanctified One, so I have heard.

' I do not say, O monks, that there is any evil deed that is incapable of being done, by an individual that hath transgressed a (certain) single Law.' ' What Law?' ' Just this, O monks— the Law (against) intentional falsehood (*sampajāna-musāvāda-*).'

To this effect spake the Blessed One, and hereupon said the following:

'Of one that hath transgressed that one Law
(Which forbiddeth) Falsehood, and that is
Unmindful of the future world—of him
There is no sin undone.'

Exactly to that effect was it spoken by the Blessed One, so I have heard.

§ 26. This verily was said by the Blessed One, said by the Sanctified One, so I have heard.

' Creatures should know the result, O monks, of the distribution of charity (lit. gifts), just as I know it; they should not eat without having given; and the stain of selfishness should not make its deep impression on their hearts. Whatever least bit or morsel they may have, if there should be anyone to receive of it, they should not eat without first having shared. And since, moreover, O monks, creatures do not know the result of the distribution of charity, as I know it—for this reason, they eat without having first given, and the stain of selfishness hath made its deep impression on their hearts.'

To this effect spake the Blessed One, and hereupon said the following:

' If creatures should know
(Just as the Great Sage hath said),
What wondrous fruit
Cometh from giving gifts

Having with undisturbéd mind
Put away all stain of selfishness
They would give proper gifts to the deserving;
From this act there cometh (to them) great reward.

And having given much[1] food
As a gift to the deserving,[2]
Benefactors, when they leave
This human life (*manussatta-*), do go to heaven.

And those that have gone to heaven
Rejoice there in bliss[3];
(And) losing their selfishness, they enjoy
The result of generosity.'

Exactly to that effect was it spoken by the Blessed One, so I have heard.

§ 27. This verily was said by the Blessed One, said by the Sanctified One, so I have heard.

' Whatsoever materials there are, O monks, for the acquisition of Virtue (*puñña-kiriya-vatthu-*), connected with the Substrata,[4]

---

[1] *bahuno*, a gen. sing., shows a transfer to the consonant declension; see Henry, *Grammaire Pâlie*, § 170, notes 1 and 2.

[2] *dakkhineyyesu;* for the loc. case used in the sense of a dat. in Sanskrit, see Speyer, *Sanskrit Syntax*, § 145.

[3] *kāmakāmina-;* lit. ' rejoicing in love,' a compound usually employed in a bad sense.

[4] *upadhi-;* this term presents one of the most difficult problems to the translator. Childers, *Pāli Dict.*, defines it as ' a wheel; the body; substratum of being.' He notes also that there are four varieties of *upadhi*, namely, the *khandhas*, ' Attributes,' *Kāma*, ' Lust,' *kilesa*, ' depravity, defilement,' and *kamma*, ' moral merit, Karma.' As a rendering I have chosen ' Substratum,' and it occurs in §§ 51, 73, 77, 112. For further discussion see Müller, *The Dhammapāda, SBE.* 10, note on verse 418. Compare also my reference at page 57, note 2, below.

Connected in meaning with *upadhi-*, is the word *upādi-*, occurring usually in all these do not equal a sixteenth part (the value) of Friendliness (*mettā-*),[1] (which is) an emancipation of the thoughts (*ceto-vimutti-*); for Friendliness, verily, an emancipation of the thoughts, transcending (everything),[2] doth shine, and glow, and radiate.

'Just as, O monks, whatever may be the light (*pabhā-*) of the starry forms, all (together) do not equal a sixteenth part of the light of the moon, for the latter, verily, transcending them, doth shine, and glow, and radiate; even so, O monks, whatsoever materials there may be for the acquisition of Virtue, connected with the Substrata, all these do not equal a sixteenth part (the value) of Friendliness, (which is) an emancipation of the thoughts; for Friendliness, verily, emancipation of the thoughts, transcending (everything), doth shine, and glow, and radiate.

'Just as, O monks, in the last month of the rainy season, in autumn time, when the sky is clear[3] and the clouds have rifted (*vigata-*), the sun, ascending the sky and pervading all that is situate either in light or in darkness, doth shine, and glow, and radiate; even so, O monks, whatsoever materials there may be for the acquisition of Virtue, connected with the Substrata, all these do not equal a sixteenth part (the value) of Friendliness, (which is) an emancipation of the thoughts; for Friendliness, verily, emancipation of the thoughts, transcending (everything), doth shine, and glow, and radiate.

'Just as, O monks, at night when the dawn draweth near, the morning-star[4] doth shine, and glow, and radiate; even so,

the compound *upādisesa-*, 'having the Substrata remaining'; this compound occurs in §§ 44, 45, 46, and 47 of this work. The etymology of *upādi-* is not certain; Childers compares it with Skt. *up-ā-dā-.* He notes that the Northern Buddhists frequently confuse the two words.

[1] This characteristic of perfect kindliness will be exemplified in Meteyya, the coming Buddha. The word *mettā-* is sometimes rendered 'love,' but I prefer to translate literally, comparing with Skt. *maitra-,* 'a friend.'

[2] *adhi-gahetvā;* this compound of the root *grabh-,* 'to seize,' does not occur in Sanskrit. Pischel, who has translated the prose of this section, *Leben und Lehre des Buddha,* p. 78, renders this word 'nimmt sie in sich auf.'

[3] MS. S reads *viddhe,* Skt. *vyadh-, vidh-,* 'pierced.'

[4] *osadhi-tārakā;* lit. 'the star presiding over medicine.' See Childers, *Pāli Dict.,* s. v. The same epithet occurs in Sinhalese, v. Clough, *Sinh. Dict.*

O monks, whatsoever materials there may be for the acquisition of Virtue, connected with the Substrata, all these do not equal a sixteenth part (the value) of Friendliness, (which is) an emancipation of the thoughts; for Friendliness, verily, an emancipation of the thoughts, transcending (everything), doth shine, and glow, and radiate.'

To this effect spake the Blessed One, and hereupon said the following:

'Few are the Fetters of him
That doth see the destruction of the Substrata;
Who is thoughtful, and who doth possess
Boundless (*appamāna-*) Friendliness.

If one doth act in friendly wise,
With no evil thought toward any single creature,
And in so doing becometh proper,
And if he have compassion in his soul (*manas-*, lit. mind)
Toward all living beings—this noble one
Doth acquire abundant Virtue.

Those royal sages (*rājīsayo*), who, after conquering
The earth with its myriads of creatures,
Have gone round it offering sacrifice[1]
(The Horse Sacrifice, the Human Sacrifice,[2] the *Sammā-
pāsa* Sacrifice,[3]

---

[1] *anupariyagā*, Skt. *anu-pary-ā-gam-;* which Böhtlingk and Roth define as 'durchgehen, durchwandern,' citing only one instance of its occurrence, *viz.*, Mahābhārata, 12.223.24, Bombay edit., or 12.8081, Calcutta edit. This MBh. passage reads *yadā ca pṛthivīm sarvām yajamāno 'nuparyagāh*, 'formerly, engaged in sacrifice, thou hadst gone around all the earth,' etc. See Rāy, *Translation of the Mahābhārata*, Calcutta, 1891, vol. 11, p. 195.

It seems to me conclusive that our Pāli text contains here a quotation from the Sanskrit. Not only in both cases do we have the rare word *anupariyagā* immediately following *yajamāna*, 'sacrificing,' but the entire passage is remarkably similar in both.

[2] These sacrifices seem likewise a reminiscence of the Mahābhārata; see Hopkins, *Great Epic*, pp. 377 ff., and 474.

[3] *sammāpāsam;* Childers defines this word as 'one of the four great sacrifices, Hindu, not Buddhist. He gives no etymology. Professor Jackson

The *Vājapeyya* Sacrifice unrestrainedly[1]—),[2]
Are not equal to the sixteenth part of a heart (*citta-*) well
trained and kindly.[3]

He that killeth not, and causeth not to kill[4]
Who doth not injure, and who causeth not to injure[5]
Hath the friendship of all creatures;
There is no wrath at him for any cause.'

Exactly to that effect was it spoken by the Blessed One, so I
have heard.

Résumé 3

Contemplative in heart (§ 21)[6]; the two welfares (§ 23);
Virtue (§ 22)[7]; huge mountain (§ 24)[8];
Intentional falsehood (§ 25);

suggests comparing *sammāpāsa-* with Skt. *śamyāprāsa-*, in connection with the
rājasūya sacrifice; compare Weber, *Über den rājasūya, Abh. der Berl. Akad.*,
July, 1893, p. 85, note 5; see also Monier Williams, *Skt. Dict.*, s. v. Subhūti,
Abhidhānappadīpikā, § 413, includes it among 'the five great sacrifices.'

[1] *niraggalam*, Skt. *nir-argala*. Clough, *Sinhalese Dictionary*, p. 292, says
this was 'one of the four great sacrifices'; Subhūti, *Abhidhānappadīpikā*,
§ 413, includes it among 'the five great sacrifices.' In my judgment both are
in error. Literally the word means, 'without a bolt, unrestrained, unbarred,'
and secondarily, 'unhindered, freely,' these being the meanings in Sanskrit.

[2] These two lines, which are put in parentheses in Windisch's edition, are
found also in a somewhat different connection in the *Samyutta Nikāya*, ed. by
Léon Feer, *PTS.* vol. i, p. 76.

[3] Directly after this six-line stanza is the following verse; *chandappabhā
tāraganā va sabbe.* Windisch puts it in parentheses, and thinks it an old
interpolation. On merely metrical reasons it is certainly an interloper; the
words, which mean 'as all the groups of stars the radiance of the moon,'
have no apparent connection with the verses preceding. It is possible that
this verse crept in from the prose portion of this section.

[4] *ghāteti*, caus. of *han-*, 'to kill.'

[5] *jināti*, Skt. *jyā-*.

[6] Not *cittam jhāyī*, but rather *pasanna-citta-*, 'tranquil in heart,' are the
words of the text.

[7] Observe the misplacement of the résumés of §§ 22, 23, for metrical
reasons.

[8] This is an emphatic word in § 24, but it does not appear to me to be
particularly appropriate as a key-word for the passage.

Both giving (§ 26) ; and the state of Friendship (§ 27).[56]
All these stanzas (*sutta-*)
And the twenty preceding ones
Are stanzas (*suttanta-*)[2] about divers laws.
(In all, they are) twenty-seven sections.

End of the first division.

SECOND DIVISION

§ 28. This verily was said by the Blessed One, said by the Sanctified One, so I have heard.

'By being possessed of two things, O monks, doth a monk live in this world in Misery, with its vexation, its despair, and its distress, and after the dissolution of the body after death, Misfortune awaiteth him.' 'What are these two things?' 'By not guarding the door to the senses[3] and by intemperance[4] in eating. By being possessed of these two things, O monks, a monk doth live in this world in Misery, with its vexation, its despair, and its distress, and after the dissolution of the body after death, Misfortune awaiteth him.'

To this effect spake the Blessed One, and hereupon said the following:

> 'Sight, hearing, and smell,
> 　　Taste, touch, and consciousness—
> 　　Whatsoever monk here (in this world)
> 　　Hath these doors unguarded,
>
> He, being intemperate in eating,
> 　　Unrestrained in his senses,
> 　　Attaineth unto Misery,
> 　　Of body and soul[5] alike.

---

[1] The words *bhāva-*, 'condition,' and *ca—ca*, 'both—and,' are added metri gratia.

[2] The two different words both meaning stanza are used for metrical reasons. See Subhūti, *Pāli Dictionary*, where *suttanta* is glossed by *sutta*.

[3] See page 71, note 4.

[4] *amattaññutā-;* lit. 'the quality of being unfamiliar with moderation.' This compound is not cited by Böhtlingk and Roth in Sanskrit.

[5] *cetas-;* lit. 'thought.'

> Such a one doth live in Misery
> Whether it be by day or by night,
> Inflamed in body
> 'And inflamed in soul.'

Exactly to that effect was it spoken by the Blessed One, so I have heard.

§ 29. This verily was said by the Blessed One, said by the Sanctified One, so I have heard.

'By being possessed of two things, O monks, doth a monk live in this world in happiness, with its lack of vexation, its lack of despair, and its lack of distress, and after the dissolution of the body after death, felicity awaiteth him.' 'What are these two things?' 'By guarding the door to the senses, and by temperance in eating. By being possessed of these two things, O monks, doth a monk live in this world in happiness, with its lack of vexation, its lack of despair, its lack of distress, and after the dissolution of the body after death, felicity awaiteth him.'

To this effect spake the Blessed One, and hereupon said the following:

> 'Sight, hearing, and smell,
> Taste, touch, and consciousness—
> Whatsoever monk here (in this world)
> Hath these doors guarded,

> He, being temperate in eating,
> Restrained in his senses,
> Attaineth unto happiness,
> Of body and soul alike.

> Such a one doth live in happiness
> Whether it be by day or by night,
> Uninflamed in body
> And uninflamed in soul.'

Exactly to that effect was it spoken by the Blessed One, so I have heard.

§ 30. This verily was said by the Blessed One, said by the Sanctified One, so I have heard.

'There are these two things, O monks, which give (me) pain.' 'What two?' 'There is here, O monks, a certain man that hath not done (acts) that are good and righteous, who hath not given protection to those that are afraid, and who hath done (acts) that are hard-hearted[1] and guilty. The goodness which he hath not done doth cause me pain, and the evil which he hath done, doth cause me pain.[2] These are the two things, O monks, which cause me pain.'

To this effect spake the Blessed One, and hereupon said the following:

'He that hath sinned
In body, word, or thought,
Or in anything
That is called sinful,

Doing not that which is righteous,
But doing much that is unrighteous—
This fool after the dissolution of the body,
Shall go to perdition.'

Exactly to that effect was it spoken by the Blessed One, so I have heard.

§ 31. This verily was said by the Blessed One, said by the Sanctified One, so I have heard.

'There are these two things, O monks, which give (me) no pain.' 'What two?' 'There is here, O monks, a certain man that hath done (acts) that are good and righteous, who hath given protection to those that are afraid, and who hath not done (acts) that are hard-hearted and guilty. The goodness which he hath done, doth cause me no pain, and the evil which he hath not done, doth not cause me pain. These are the two things, O monks, which do not cause me pain.'

---

[1] *thaddha-*, Skt. *stabdha-;* in his fifth subdivision under this latter word, Apte, *Skt. Dict.*, renders 'hard-hearted, cruel, stern.'

[2] Sins of omission, and sins of commission.

To this effect was it spoken by the Blessed One, so I have heard.

'He that avoideth sin
In body, word, and thought,
Or anything that is called sinful,
Doing much that is righteous,
But not doing that which is unrighteous—
This virtuous man, after the dissolution of the body, shall
    go to heaven.'

Exactly to that effect was it spoken by the Blessed One, so I have heard.

§ 32. This verily was said by the Blessed One, said by the Sanctified One, so I have heard.

'An individual is cast into perdition, O monks, by being possessed of two qualities as is handed down by tradition.'[1] 'What two?' 'Evil character (*pāpaka-sīla-*) and evil Belief. An individual by being possessed of these two qualities, O monks, is cast into perdition, as is handed down by tradition.'

To this effect spake the Blessed One, and hereupon said the following:

'That man that is possessed
Of the two evil qualities
Of evil character and evil Belief,
Is a wicked man,
Who, after the dissolution of the body,
Shall go to perdition.'

Exactly to that effect was it spoken by the Blessed One, so I have heard.

§ 33. This verily was said by the Blessed One, said by the Sanctified One, so I have heard.

'An individual is translated[2] into heaven, O monks, by being possessed of two qualities, as is handed down by tradition.' 'What two?' 'Upright character and upright Belief. An indi-

---

[1] See page 32, note 2.

[2] *nikkhitta-*, lit. 'cast into,' as in § 32 above.

vidual by being possessed of these two qualities, O monks, is translated into heaven, as is handed down by tradition.'

To this effect spake the Blessed One, and hereupon said the following:

> ' That man that is possessed
> Of the two upright qualities
> Of upright character and upright Belief,
> Is a virtuous man, who,
> After the dissolution of the body,
> Shall go to heaven.'

Exactly to that effect was it spoken by the Blessed One, so I have heard.

§ 34. This verily was said by the Blessed One, said by the Sanctified One, so I have heard.

' A slothful, froward[1] monk is unfit for Supreme Enlightenment, O monks, is unfit for Nirvāna, is unfit for the attainment of the Supreme Security[2]; but the monk that is ardent, O monks, and not froward, is fit for Supreme Enlightenment, is fit for Nirvāna, and is fit for the attainment of the Supreme Security.'

To this effect spake the Blessed One, and hereupon said the following:

> ' A monk, who is slothful and froward,
> Indolent and feeble,
> Who hath much idleness and laziness,
> Who is shameless and disrespectful—
> Such a monk is unfit
> To attain Supreme Enlightenment.
>
> He that is thoughtful, prudent,[3] and reflective,
> Fervent, not froward, and earnest,

---

[1] *anottappa-;* see Mrs. Rhys Davids, *DhS.* p. 20, and *SBE.* 9. 8. *ottappa-* means ' fear of censure, dread of reproach, decency in outward behavior.'

[2] See page 30, note 1.

[3] *nipaka-;* the etymology of this word is doubtful; it is perhaps comparable to Skt. *pac-,* ' to cook,' hence, ' ripe, mature, drinking in knowledge, receptive.' It occurs also in §§ 45, 47, 93, 37 c.

Hath destroyed his Fetters of Birth and Death;
He may attain Supreme Enlightenment e'en here (on
earth).'

Exactly to that effect was it spoken by the Blessed One, so I
have heard.

§ 35. This verily was said by the Blessed One, said by the
Sanctified One, so I have heard.

'People should know me, O monks, as saying that the life of
chastity (*brahma-cariya-*) is not lived for the purpose of deceiving or prating to mankind, nor for the sake of the advantage
(*ānisaṃsa-*) of a reputation (*siloka-*) for gain and one's own
affairs[1]; but as saying that this life of chastity is lived, O
monks, for the purpose of Restraint and Renunciation
(*pahāna-*).'

To this effect spake the Blessed One, and hereupon said the
following:

'The Blessed One hath pointed out
That a life of chastity without traditional instruction,[2]
With the goal of Restraint (*saṃvara-*) and
Renunciation, is the road that leadeth[3] to Nirvāna.

This path is attained by great-souled sages;
All those that enter upon it,
As the Blessed One hath pointed out,

[1] *sakkāra-;* in my opinion this word is not the equivalent of Skt. *satkāra-,*
'hospitality,' as is stated in Childers, *Pāli Dict.* s. v. I compare it with Skt.
sva-, 'his, their' and *kāra-,* 'business, affair.' The doubling of the *k* is
difficult to explain; an exact parallel, however, is found in the compound
sakkāyābhiratā, 'taking delight in their own bodies,' § 93 h. The doubling of
the *k* may be in compensation for the loss of the *v* in the preceding syllable.
sakkāra- occurs again in §§ 36, 80, 81 of this work.

[2] *anītiham;* notice the hit against the brahmans. Compare R. Morris,
Notes and Queries, PTS. 1886, p. 111.

[3] *gadh-;* this root is cited by Pānini and other native grammarians, and by
Whitney, *Roots of Skt. Lang.,* but the latter questions its genuineness as not
occurring in any extant Sanskrit text. Its occurrence in Pāli confirms its
genuineness in Sanskrit. The same root occurs again in this work, in § 36
below and § 95 i. In the latter passage I have rendered 'connection.'

> Will end their Misery,
> For they carry out
> The commands of the Teacher.'

Exactly to that effect was it spoken by the Blessed One, so I have heard.

§ 36. This verily was said by the Blessed One, said by the Sanctified One, so I have heard.

'People should know me, O monks, as saying that the life of chastity is not lived for the purpose of deceiving or prating to mankind, nor for the sake of the advantage of a reputation for gain and one's own affairs; but as saying that this life of chastity is lived, O monks, for the purpose of Insight and Thorough Knowledge.'

To this effect spake the Blessed One, and hereupon said the following:

> 'The Blessed One hath pointed out
> That a life of chastity without traditional instruction,
> With the goal of Insight and Thorough Knowledge,
> Is the road which leadeth to Nirvāna.
>
> This path is attained by great-souled sages;
> All those that enter upon it,
> As the Blessed One hath pointed out,
> Will end their Misery,
> For they carry out
> The commands of the Teacher.'

Exactly to that effect was it spoken by the Blessed One, so I have heard.

§ 37. This verily was said by the Blessed One, said by the Sanctified One, so I have heard.

'A monk liveth with much happiness and enjoyment in this visible world, O monks, by being possessed of two things, and he hath begun to destroy profoundly[1] his sins.' 'What are these

---

[1] *yoniso*, Skt. *yoni-śas;* lit. 'from the womb, fundamentally.' It glosses line d of the stanza below. It is used also to gloss *vijjā-*, 'knowledge,' and *ñāna-*, 'understanding.' The same word is also used in § 16.

two things?' 'By being cautious in matters requiring caution,[1] and by striving profoundly for spiritual power.[2] A monk doth live with much happiness and enjoyment in this visible world by being possessed of these two things, and he hath begun to destroy profoundly his sins.'

To this effect spake the Blessed One, and hereupon said the following:

'A wise man should be cautious
In places requiring caution.
A fervent, prudent monk,
Reflecting with wisdom.

Thus living fervent, reposeful in manner,
Not vaunting himself[3]
Possessed of tranquillity of soul (*cetas-*),
He may attain unto the destruction of Misery.'

Exactly to that effect was it spoken by the Blessed One, so I have heard.

[End of] first chapter [of second division]

Résumé 4

These two (about a) monk (§§ 28, 29)[4]; painful
And Pleasant (things) (§§ 30, 31); by opposite qualities
    (§§ 32, 33)[5];
A fervent (one) (§ 34)[6]; and (two on) non-deception (§§ 35, 36);

---

[1] *samvejana-*, Skt. *sam-vij-*, 'to tremble.' There is evidently a play on words between this word and *samvega-*.

[2] *samvega-*; Böhtlingk and Roth define this word in Sanskrit as 'eine heftige Gemütsaufregung, Heftigkeit, Gewalt.'

[3] Literally, 'not puffed up.'

[4] In both of these stanzas *indriya*, 'sense,' not *bhikku*, is the important key word.

[5] Indefinite for good and bad *sīla-* and *diṭṭhi-*, 'character and Belief.'

[6] *ātāpi*, absent in all MSS. except S. The word *anottapi*, 'not froward,' would be expected rather than *ātāpi*, as it comes first in the text.

By enjoyment (§ 37)[1].; these ten.[2]

§ 38. This verily was said by the Blessed One, said by the Sanctified One, so I have heard.

'Two ideas,[3] O monks, greatly concern the Consummate One, the Sanctified One, the Supremely Enlightened One: the idea of Security (*khema-*) and the idea of Solitude (*paviveka-*). For the Consummate One, O monks, delighteth in and is delighted by Non-injury.[4] This particular idea much concerneth the Consummate One, delighting in and delighted by Non-injury, viz., " By this deportment I cause no injury to animate or inanimate life."[5]

'The Consummate One, O monks, delighteth in and is delighted by Solitude. This particular idea much concerneth the Consummate One, delighting in and delighted by Solitude, viz., "Whatever is wicked hath been forsaken."

'Therefore do ye live, O monks, delighting in and delighted by Non-injury. For those of you, O monks, who live delighting in and delighted by Non-injury, this particular idea will be of great concern, viz., " By this deportment we cause no injury to animate or inanimate life." Therefore likewise, O monks, do ye live, delighting in and delighted by Solitude. For those of you, O monks, who live delighting in and delighted by Solitude, this particular idea is of great concern, viz., "Whatsoever is wicked hath been forsaken."'

---

[1] The important word of the section is not this, but *samvejanīyesu thānesu,* 'in matters requiring caution.' *somanassa,* ' enjoyment,' is put in the instr. case metri gratia.

[2] The résumé of these ten sections (28–37) is given again after § 49 below, with, however, considerable variations.

[3] *vitakka-;* Mrs. Rhys Davids *DhS.* §§ 7, 160, 166, 263, 283, 441 a, 461, renders ' conception.' As I translate *citta-* by ' thought,' I prefer here to render ' idea.'

[4] *abyābajjha-;* cf. Skt. root *bādh-,* ' to injure.' In Skt. the root is not compounded with the preps. here in the Pāli word, namely, *a, vi, ā.* We find here apparently the *Ahiṃsa* doctrine which is especially characteristic of the Jain religion.

[5] *tasam vā thāvaram vā;* lit. ' moving and stationary.'

To this effect spake the Blessed One, and hereupon said the following:

'Two ideas greatly concern the Consummate One,
Buddha, he that endureth the unendurable.
The first (of these) is called Security,
The second is called Seclusion (*viveka-*).

That great Sage who hath dispelled darkness, who hath
    crossed the Flood,
Who is self-subdued, and freed from the Taints,[1]
He hath gained the highest Gain.
That man, wholly emancipated

By destruction of Thirst, I declare
(To be) a saint that hath put on his final body,
That hath abandoned Pride
And passed beyond Old Age.

Even as one standing on a mountain top
May see rocks and mankind on every side,
Just so the well-known Sumedha,
Having ascended the Highest Dharma, like a palace (roof),
Casting his glance on every side, looketh down with grief
    departed,
On mankind immersed in grief, and overcome by Birth and
    Old Age.'

Exactly to that effect was it spoken by the Blessed One, so I have heard.

§ 39. This verily was said by the Blessed One, said by the Sanctified One, so I have heard.

'The Consummate One, the Sanctified One, the Supremely Enlightened One, O monks, hath given[2] these two commandments, the one higher than the other.'[3] 'What two?' '"Let

---

[1] See page 65, note 2.
[2] Literally 'Of the Sanctified One, etc., there are these two commandments.'
[3] *pariyāyā-;* the same use of the instr. case of this word occurs in Skt.

Sin (*pāpa-*) be beheld from the standpoint of its sinfulness";
this is the first commandment. "And when ye have thus beheld
Sin, be ye disgusted at it, loathe it, and become freed from it."
These, O monks, are the two commandments, the one higher than
the other, as given by the Consummate One, the Sanctified One,
the Supremely Enlightened One.'

To this effect spake the Blessed One, and hereupon said the
following:

> 'Behold the Word (*vacana-*) and the manner (of its pres-
>   entation),
> The two recognized commandments
> Of the Consummate One, the Buddha,
> Compassionate to all creatures.
>
> Look on Sin and loathe it;
> With minds loathing it,
> Then will ye make
> An end of Misery.'

Exactly to that effect was it spoken by the Blessed One, so I
have heard.

§ 40. This verily was said by the Blessed One, said by the
Sanctified One, so I have heard.

'Ignorance (*avijjā-*), O monks, goeth before the performance
of wicked deeds (*dhamma-*) (lit. things); in its train[1] follow
Shamelessness and Hardness of Heart.[2]　Knowledge, O monks,
goeth before the performance of good deeds, and in the train
(of these) follow Shame and Fear of Sinning.'

To this effect spake the Blessed One, and hereupon said the
following:

> 'Whatsoever misfortunes there are
> Here in this world or in the next,
> They all have their root in Ignorance
> And in the accumulation of Longing (*icchā-*) and Desire.

---

[1] *anvad-eva;* for euphonic *d,* cf. *sammadaññā-,* in § 1 c.

[2] *anottappa-;* the opposite *ottappa-* in § 42 is rendered 'fear of sinning,' *i. e.*
sensitiveness of conscience.

And inasmuch as he hath evil Longing,
And is shameless and regardless,
For that reason he breedeth Sin,
And he goeth to punishment thereby.

Therefore by becoming emancipated from
Yearning (*chanda-*) and Desire and Ignorance,
And by acquiring knowledge,
A monk may abandon all misfortunes.'

Exactly to that effect was it spoken by the Blessed One, so I have heard.

First portion for recital

§ 41. This verily was said by the Blessed One, said by the Sanctified One, so I have heard.

' Greatly deficient, O monks, are those creatures who are deficient in holy wisdom: they dwell in Misery in this visible world, (in Misery) with its obstacles, with its impending pain, with its anguish; and after death and the dissolution of the body, misfortune awaiteth them. But those are not deficient, O monks, who are not deficient in holy wisdom, dwell in happiness in the visible world, without obstacles, without impending pain, without anguish; and after death and the dissolution of the body, felicity awaiteth them.'

To this effect spake the Blessed One, and hereupon said the following:

' It is through lack of wisdom
One thinketh that This[1] is true,
As he looketh on this world
Immersed in Name and Form.

For in the world that is the best wisdom
Which leadeth to Discrimination,
And which rightly comprehendeth
The destruction of Birth and Existence.

[1] *idam*, ' das Weltall.' The same use of the word is found in Skt.; see ref. in Böhtlingk and Roth, s. v.

Both gods and men are envious of those
Who are supremely enlightened,
Heedful, having wisdom, and who
Have put on their final body.'

Exactly to that effect was it spoken by the Blessed One, so I have heard.

§ 42. This verily was said by the Blessed One, said by the Sanctified One, so I have heard.

'These two laws, O monks, do protect the world.' 'What two?' 'Shame and Fear of Sinning. If these two laws did not protect the world, ye would not make distinction between mothers or aunts, or aunts-in-law, or the wives of preceptors (ācariya-), or the wives of teachers[1]; the world would go[2] to confusion; for example, goats with sheep, cocks with sows (1),[3] dogs with jackals. And inasmuch, indeed, as these two pure laws do protect the world, O monks, for that reason there is distinction between mothers, aunts, aunts-in-law, wives of preceptors, and wives of teachers.'

To this effect spake the Blessed One, and hereupon said the following:

'In whomsoe'er Shame and Fear of Sinning
Are found at all times,
These persons, radically pure, have passed beyond (*i. e.* the Flood),
And go no more to Birth and Death.

And further, in whomsoe'er Shame and Fear of· Sinning
Are always duly present,
These goodly people, flourishing (*virūḷha-*) in the life
Of chastity, have destroyed re-existence.'

Exactly to that effect was it spoken by the Blessed One, so I have heard.

---

[1] *garu-;* why have not mothers-in-law been included?

[2] *agamissa;* an example of the rare conditional mood. See Whitney, *Sanskrit Grammar,* § 940.

[3] *kukkuṭasūkarā-.*

§ 43. This verily was said by the Blessed One, said by the Sanctified One, so I have heard.

'There is, O monks, something not born, non-existent, not made, not compounded. If there were not this something not born, non-existent, not made, not compounded, there would not be known here deliverance from what is born, existent, made, and compounded. Since, indeed, O monks, there is something not born, non-existent, not made, and not compounded, therefore there is known deliverance from what is born, existent, made, and compounded.'

To this effect spake the Blessed One, and hereupon said the following:

> 'It is not possible to delight in That[1] which is born,
> Which has existence, is produced, is made, is com-
> pounded, unstable,
> Subject to Old Age and Death,
> A nest of diseases, fragile,[2]
> And owing its operative cause
> To the current of subsistence.[3]

> The destruction of This is a state that is tranquil,
> That hath passed beyond conjecture,
> That is not born and not produced,
> That is griefless and passionless—
> The annihilation of the conditions of Misery,
> A happy cessation of Doubt.'

Exactly to that effect was it spoken by the Blessed One, so I have heard.

§ 44. This verily was said by the Blessed One, said by the Sanctified One, so I have heard.

---

[1] *tad;* used after the manner of *idaṃ rupaṃ,* Dhp. § 148, representing the human body, characterized as *roga-nīla-,* 'a nest of diseases.' This latter attribute also appears in the Dhammapada, § 148.

[2] *pabhaṅgunaṃ,* Skt. *prabhaṅgana,* 'zerbrechlich'; for the *na* suffix, cf. Whitney, *Skt. Gram.* 1223 g. Fausböll has 'fragilis.'

[3] *āhāra-netti-;* cf. Skt. *āhāra,* 'subsistence,' and *netrī-,* 'a river.' Compare *nettichinna-,* § 94 b.

'There are, O monks, these two Elements[1] of Nirvāna.'
'What two?' 'The Nirvāna element of having the Substrata
(*upādi-*) still remaining, and the Nirvāna element of having the
Substrata no longer remaining.[2]

'What, O monks, is the Nirvāna Element which hath not the
Substrata remaining? A monk becometh sanctified here (in
this world), if he, while living, hath destroyed his Taints—if
he hath done that which ought to be done, if he hath laid aside
his burdens, if he hath attained good welfare, if he hath destroyed the Fetters of Existence, if he is emancipated by Perfect Knowledge. He hath five moral qualities, *viz.*, his mind
is unimpeded, he experienceth[3] what is pleasant and unpleasant,
and he cometh to know happiness and misery. His destruction
of Passion, of Anger, of Ignorance, is called the Nirvāna Element of having the Substrata remaining.

'What, O monks, is the Nirvāna Element which doth not
have the Substrata remaining? A monk becometh sanctified
here (in this world), if, while living, he hath done that which
ought to be done, if he hath laid aside his burdens, if he hath
attained good welfare, if he hath destroyed the Fetters of Existence, if he is emancipated by Perfect Knowledge. All his
feelings,[4] O monks, if not rejoiced in here (in this world) will
become cold[5]—This, O monks, is called the Nirvāna Element
of not having the Substrata remaining. These, O monks, are the
two Nirvāna Elements.'

[1] *dhātu-;* for its usage cf. Mrs. Rhys Davids, *DhS.* §§ 455, 648, 703, 1333.
[2] This mention of the partial, as well as the total separation from things
earthly, as an element, or condition, of Nirvāna, seems to lend strong confirmation to the view of the doctrine of Nirvāna advanced by Childers,
Pāli Dict., s. v. Compare my note on § 27. According to Kern, *Indian
Buddhism*, p. 50, note 2, this passage contradicts absolutely lines e and f of
the first stanza below of this section. He says that this particular prose-
passage is wrong, but that lines e and f below have the correct definition.
[3] *paccanubhoti*, Skt. *praty-anu-bhū-*, 'to suffer, bear, undergo.'
[4] *vedayitāni*, a ppl. used in place of the more common noun, *vedita-*.
[5] *sīta-*, Skt. *śita-*, 'cold.' For the change of final *a* to *ī* before *bhū-*, cf.
Whitney, *Skt. Gram.*, §§ 1092, 1093, and Franke, *Pāli und Sanskrit*, p. 103, note
72. For similar formations in the Avesta, see Bartholomae, *Altiranisches Wörterbuch*, s. v. *saoči-bhū-* and *varaθa-bhū-*.

To this effect spake the Blessed One, and hereupon said the following:

' These two Nirvāna elements have been made known by Such
   a One (*tādinā*)
As hath Spiritual Insight,—the one Element, verily, hath
A visible condition here, with Substrata (still) remaining,
(Although) the current of Existence is destroyed;
But (the other Element) having the Substrata no (longer)
   remaining,
Is future, in which state all creatures are wholly annihilated.

Those who, by having known this state which is uncom-
   pounded,
Are emancipated in (their) thoughts, and those who have
   destroyed
The current of Existence[1]—these persons have attained the
   quintessence of the Law,
And delight in Destruction.   (Such as) they have abandoned
   all Existences.'

Exactly to that effect was it spoken by the Blessed One, so I have heard.

§ 45. This verily was said by the Blessed One, said by the Sanctified One, so I have heard.

' Live, O monks, delighting in and delighted by the Recluse Life (*pāṭisallāna-*), examining into that-which-concerneth-the-inner-self,[2] which hath tranquillity of thought, not rejecting Meditation,[3] endowed with Discernment,[4] and exalting[5]

[1] Compare the note on *āhāra-netti* in the preceding section.

[2] *ajjhattaṃ*, phonetically equivalent to Skt. *ādhy-ātman-*. Mrs. Rhys Davids renders ' that which is self-evolved,' but expresses uncertainty as to the meaning; see *DhS.*, intro., p. lxxi, and §§ 161, 673, 742-4, 1044. The word is often contrasted with *bāhiraṃ* or *bahiddhā-*, ' external, objective.'

[3] *jhāna-;* for a full and excellent discussion of this important word, see Mrs. Rhys Davids, *DhS.* §§ 160, 165, 167, 170-5, 1098, 1281-7, and pp. 361-3.

[4] *vipassana-;* cf. Skt. *vi-darśana-*, and see Rhys Davids, *Questions of King Milinda, SBE.* 35, p. 25.

[5] *bruhetā-;* I take this word to be a caus. ppl., corresponding to Skt. root *bṛnh-*, ' to roar, to grow, increase'; caus. ' to nourish, to elevate.' At best the rendering is unsatisfactory.

in empty organs of sense.[1] Those who live delighting in and delighted by the Recluse Life, examining into that-which-concerns-the-inner-self, which has tranquillity of thought, not rejecting Meditation, endowed with Discernment, and exalting in empty organs of sense—they are to expect one of two rewards, either Knowledge in the visible world, or, if they have the Substrata remaining, the (state of) Not-returning (*anāgāmitā-*) (*i. e.* to this existence).'

To this effect spake the Blessed One, and hereupon said the following:

'Those who are good-minded, prudent,
Reflecting, and contemplative,
Who rightly discern the Law,
Nor look upon Lusts—

Those good persons, taking delight
In zeal (*appamāda-*), seeing danger
In pleasure (*pamāda-*), are not predestined (*abhabba-*)
To decrease (*parihāna-*), e'en in the presence of Nirvāna.'

Exactly to that effect was it spoken by the Blessed One, so I have heard.

§ 46. This verily was said by the Blessed One, said by the Sanctified One, so I have heard.

'Live, O monks, having the advantage[2] of learning, with quintessence (*sāra-*) of Emancipation (*vimutti-*), under good influence. Those who live delighting in and delighted by the advantage of learning, having higher wisdom, with quintessence

---

[1] All MSS. read *suññāgārānam*, lit. 'of empty houses,' except C, which has *suññakāranam*, lit. 'of empty sense-organs.' The former reading seems to me to be quite unsatisfactory, unless we are to twist its meaning by assigning to it a metaphorical sense. I therefore follow the reading of C, *suññakāranam*, and compare Skt. *karana-*, 'sense-organ.' This latter meaning can be brought into connection with *kāmesu*, 'lusts,' in line d below. For abl. use of the gen. cf. Speyer, *Sanskrit Syntax*, § 125.

[2] *ānisamsā-;* this I analyze as equivalent to Skt. **ā-ni-śams-*. This form is not cited in Böhtlingk and Roth or in Böhtlingk, but is found in Sinhalese, with the meaning 'gain, reward, profit.'

of Emancipation, under good influence—they are to expect one
of two rewards, either knowledge in the visible world, or, if one
have the Substrata remaining, the (state of) Not-returning.'

To this effect spake the Blessed One, and hereupon said the
following:

'One who is a novitiate-monk who hath not forsaken the
Law,
Who hath highest wisdom, and hath seen the end of the de-
struction of Birth—
That one, verily, I proclaim to be a saint who hath put on
His final body, and who hath abandoned Pride, and passed
beyond Old Age.

Therefore, being always delighted by Contemplation, self-
controlled, and fervent,
Seeing the end of the destruction of Birth,
(Ye have), O monks, o'ercome Death with his army,
And ye are escaped from Birth and Death.'

Exactly to that effect was it spoken by the Blessed One, so I
have heard.

§ 47. This verily was said by the Blessed One, said by the
Sanctified One, so I have heard.

'A monk should live, O monks, watchful, thoughtful, mindful,
self-composed, cheerful (*pamudita-*), both serene[1] under those
circumstances (*tattha*), and seeing the time[2] for good laws.[3]

[1] *vippasanna-*, Skt. *vi-pra-sad-*. In Skt. only *pra-sad-* is found, meaning
'to calm, soothe, appease, propitiate.' The double prefix occurs in Sinhalese,
the verb having the meaning 'to please, delight, gratify.'

[2] *kāla-vipassi-;* the second term of this compound is apparently used in
the sense of the simple form *passati*, 'to see,' and not in the sense of 'to
introspect' as in § 45, 4. Observe that *vipassi-* is here used to gloss *parivīmamsamāno* in verse g below. The latter verb is used in the comm. on the
Dhp. verse 379, to gloss *patimāseti*, 'to explore, to search.'

[3] Note the use of a plur. loc. to gloss the sing. acc. *dhammam* of verse
g below. The adj. *kusalesu*, 'good,' is used, we note, to gloss *sammā* of
verse g, which word, however, is used adverbially, since it modifies not
dhammam, but the ppl. *parivīmamsamāno*. Note also the fact that line g,

A monk that liveth watchful, thoughtful, mindful, self-composed, O monks, cheerful, serene under those circumstances, seeing the time for good laws—he is to expect one of two rewards, either knowledge in the visible world, or, if he have the Substrata remaining, the (state of) Non-returning.'

To this effect spake the Blessed One, and hereupon said the following:

'Hearken unto this, ye watchful;
Whosoever of you be asleep, let him awake.
Watchfulness is better than sleep;
The watchful one hath naught to fear.

And he that is watchful, heedful, mindful,
Self-composed, cheerful, and serene,
He rightly searcheth the Law, at the proper time[1];
Being concentrated[2] he may overcome darkness.

Therefore, in sooth, ye shall put darkness to flight.
(For) the fervent, prudent, contemplative monk,
Having cut the Fetters of Birth and Old Age,
May attain even here (in this world) Supreme Enlightenment.'

Exactly to that effect was it spoken by the Blessed One, so I have heard.

§ 48. This verily was said by the Blessed One, said by the Sanctified One, so I have heard.

'There are, O monks, these two (kinds of) men who suffer in the realm of punishment[3] and in perdition, because they have

kālena so sammā dhammam parivimamsamāno, has fifteen syllables, although it occurs in a Jagatī stanza, consisting of verses of twelve syllables each. These facts seem to me to prove that the verse is corrupt, and that it was not understood by the commentator.

[1] kālena (instr. case). This case in Skt. usually indicates 'in the course of time, during a long time, after a long time.'

[2] ekodibhūto; for a valuable discussion of this rare word, see Morris, Notes and Queries, JPTS. 1885, p. 32 ff., and cf. Mrs. Rhys Davids, DhS. § 161.

[3] apāya-; see Warren, Buddhism, p. 289–291.

not forsaken this (sin).' 'What two (kinds of men)?' 'The religious student,[1] who, after taking his vows, does not preserve his state of chastity, and (secondly) that one who, by his baseless breaking of his religious vows (of chastity), causeth the fall of one that is performing his religious vow with virtue and purity (lit. his pure and virtuous vow).'

To this effect spake the Blessed One, and hereupon said the following : ·

> ' He that speaketh falsehood goeth to perdition,
> And he that, after having done, saith " I have not done "—
> These two are equal after death,
> (For) in the other world they become men with evil deeds.

> Many whose shoulders are covered
> With the yellow gown, are ill-conditioned
> And unrestrained; such evil-doers
> By their evil deeds go to perdition.

> Better would it be to swallow a heated iron ball,
> Like flaring fire, than that a bad,
> Unrestrained fellow should live
> On the charity of the land.'[2]

Exactly to that effect was it spoken by the Blessed One, so I have heard.

§ 49. This verily was said by the Blessed One, said by the Sanctified One, so I have heard.

' As to gods and men, O monks, circumscribed[3] by two varieties of Belief,[4] some cleave to and some pass beyond[5] (Existence), and the wise behold (or, those with eyes see).' 'How

---

[1] *brahmacārī*, ' one who has taken vows,' especially vows of Chastity.

[2] Same as § 91 e–h, and Dhp. § 308.

[3] *pariyuṭṭhita-*, Skt. **pary-ud-sthita-*. Childers translates ' arisen, possessed.' This comp. does not appear in Skt. Böhtlingk and Roth translate *pari-sthā-* as ' umstehen, hindern.'

[4] *diṭṭhi-*, Skt. *dṛṣṭi-*, lit. ' sight, speculation.' Mrs. Rhys Davids, *DhS.*, §§ 257, 258, 293, 325, 342, says " heresy " is a wrong translation of this word, because there is ' sound or good *diṭṭhi-*, as well as the contrary.'

[5] *atidhāvanti;* a Vedic word, RV. 9, 3, 2, and AV. 5, 8, 4. Böhtlingk and Roth translate ' hinrinnen über, vorüberlaufen.'

is it that some cleave?' 'As to Gods and men,—O monks, delighting in and delighted by Existence (*bhava-*), and overjoyed thereby—their mind, when the law for the destruction of Existence is pointed out, doth neither spring forward, nor is it placid, neither is it settled, nor is it subject to propensity. Thus, verily, some cleave (to Existence).

'"How is it that some pass beyond?" Some, feeling reproach,[1] shame, and loathing for Existence, take delight in Cessation of Existence (*vibhava-*). Since this substance (*attha-*), Sir,[2] is destroyed and perisheth after the dissolution of the body after death, and doth not exist after death, with the idea that this (truth) is good, excellent, and seemly, certain (men) pass beyond.

'"How is it that those with eyes see?" A monk here seeth what is (*bhūtam*) from what hath been (*bhūtato*), and from this he hath attained to disgust and aversion for Existence, and repression of Existence. Thus it is, O monks, that those that have eyes see.'

To this effect spake the Blessed One, and hereupon said the following:

> 'Those having seen what is from what hath been,
> And the means of passing beyond Existence—
> They, in very truth are emancipated
> From the ruin caused by Thirst for Existence.
>
> And if one have exact knowledge of Being,
> And have quenched the Thirst for Existence and Non-
>   existence
> This monk through Cessation of Existence
> Attaineth not Rebirth.'

Exactly to that effect was it spoken by the Blessed One, so I have heard.

End of the second division[3]

---

[1] *attiyamāna-*, denom. of *ṛti-*, 'censure.'
[2] Why the sing. *bho,* instead of the common *bhikkhave?*
[3] Omitted by S.

Résumé 5

Two concerning the " senses " (§§ 28, 29) ; two on "painful"
(things) (§§ 30, 31) ;

The next two on Conduct (§§ 32, 33) ;

(A) froward (monk) (§ 34)[1]; and two on Deception (§§ 35,
36)[2];

By cautious (§ 37)[3]; these ten.

Ideas (§ 38); commandments (§ 39); knowledge (§ 40);

Wisdom (§ 41); by the Law (§ 42); (these) five[4];

The Unborn (§ 43); Element (§ 44)[5]; (Sol-)itude (§ 45)[6];

Learning (§ 46); and by Watchfulness (§ 47)[7];

Realm of punishment (§ 48); and by Belief (§ 49).[8]

These twenty-two are revealed.

FIRST CHAPTER OF THE THIRD DIVISION OF THE ITI-VUTTAKA[9]

§ 50. This verily was said by the Blessed One, said by the
Sanctified One, so I have heard.

'There are, O monks, these three sources of Impropriety
(*akusala-*).' 'What three?' 'Desire, Hate and Delusion, O
monks, are sources of Impropriety; these, verily, O monks, are
the three sources of Impropriety.

To this effect spake the Blessed One, and hereupon said the
following:

> 'Desire, Hate, and Delusion,
> Sprung from the mind,

---

[1] We might rather expect the first word of the stanza, *anātāpī*, to be chosen.

[2] The previous résumé (see p. 50) has 'non-deception' in this place.

[3] Note the sing. instead of the plur., the omission of the substantive, and
the instr. case metri gratia.

[4] This word is a 'filler,' or device to give the line the requisite number
of syllables.

[5] Notice the stem form *dhatu-*, instead of the nom. case.

[6] The first four letters of the text word, *pātisallānam*, 'Solitude,' are
omitted.

[7] Instr. case, metri gratia.

[8] Instr. case, metri gratia.

[9] This heading is inserted by S.

Destroy the man of wicked thoughts,
Like a bamboo-tree[1] with its fruit.'

Exactly to that effect was it spoken by the Blessed One, so I
have heard.

§ 51. This verily was said by the Blessed One, said by the
Sanctified One, so I have heard.

'There are these three Elements (*dhātu-*), O monks.' 'What
three?' 'The Element of Form (*rūpa-*), the Element of the
Absence of Form (*arūpa-*), and the Element of Cessation
(*nirodha-*); these verily, O monks, are the three Elements.'

To this effect spake the Blessed One, and hereupon said the
following:

'Those who, through the comprehension of the Element of
   Form,
Are not stablished in formless things,
(And) who are emancipated through Cessation—
These persons have abandoned death.

He that hath attained with his body
The immortal Element of getting-rid-of-the-Substrata (*nirū-
   padhi-*)
And who, free from Taint,[2]
Hath experienced the getting-rid-of-the-Substrata—
He, a Perfectly Enlightened One, pointeth out the Path
Which is without grief and free from Passion.'

---

[1] *tacasāra-*, Skt. *tvacsāra-*, lit. 'best of barks.'

[2] *anāsava-*, Skt. *ana-*, neg. prefix, and *āsrava-*, from root *sru-*. Monier
Williams, *Skt. Dict.*, s. v., says 'the Jainas use the word to denote the action
of the senses which impels the soul toward external objects.' It means apparently both the impulse and the resultant contamination. Childers gives a
four-fold category of *āsavas*, or 'taints,' viz., Lust, *kāma-*; Existence, *bhava-*;
Belief, *diṭṭhi-*; Ignorance, *avijjā-*.

For a discussion of the word, see Mrs. Rhys Davids, *DhS.* § 1096, and
Rhys Davids, *Dial. of Buddha*, p. 92. The word has been variously rendered,
'Deadly Floods,' 'Intoxicants,' 'Illusion (Wahn),' and 'Defilement (souillure).'
The rendering 'Taint' or 'Contamination,' will perhaps best convey the mean-
ing. Compare other occurrences of the word in §§ 38, 44, 56, 57, 59, 66, 67, 73,
96, 102, of this work. For a recurrence of these two stanzas see § 73.

Exactly to that effect was it spoken by the Blessed One, so I have heard.

§ 52. This verily was said by the Blessed One, said by the Sanctified One, so I have heard.

'There are, O monks, these three feelings (*vedana-*).' 'What three?' 'Pleasant feelings, painful feelings, and feelings which are neither pleasant nor painful. These verily, O monks, are the three feelings.'

To this effect spake the Blessed One, and hereupon said the following:

> 'The self-composed, mindful,
> And thoughtful disciple of Buddha,
> Comprehendeth the feelings,
> And the cause of the feelings,
>
> And comprehendeth where they cease,
> And the Path that leadeth to destruction (*khaya-gāmina-*).
> By the destruction of (his) feelings,
> This monk hath extinguished Hunger,[1] and hath attained
> Nirvāna.'

Exactly to that effect was it spoken by the Blessed One, so I have heard.

§ 53. This verily was said by the Blessed One, said by the Sanctified One, so I have heard.

'There are these three Feelings, O monks.' 'What three?' 'Pleasant feelings, painful feelings, and feelings which are neither pleasant nor painful. A pleasant feeling, O monks, is to be recognized from (its) pain, a painful feeling from (its) pang (*sallato*), (while) a feeling which is neither pleasant nor painful is to be recognized from (its) not lasting.

'Since indeed, O monks, a pleasant feeling experienced by a monk becometh recognized from its pain, and a painful feeling becometh recognized from its pang, (and) a feeling which is

---

[1] *nicchāta-;* the comm. as cited by Windisch, glosses this word by *nittaṇha-*, 'absence of Thirst.' It is probably from the rare Skt. root *psā-*, 'to hunger,' with the privative prefix *nir-*, or *nis-*. The last four lines are identical with the third stanza of § 73.

neither pleasant nor painful becometh recognized from (its) not lasting—that monk is called noble, O monks, and correct in his views, one that hath eradicated Thirst, and one that causeth the removal[1] of the Fetters; for his comprehension of rightful purposes he hath made an end of Misery.'

To this effect spake the Blessed One, and hereupon said the following:

> 'Whatsoever monk hath recognized pleasure
> From (its) pain, and pain from (its) pang,
> And hath recognized from (its) not lasting, the presence
> Of the (state) which is neither pleasant nor painful,
>
> This monk verily hath proper vision (*sammādasa-*)
> Inasmuch as he is emancipated here (in this world);
> If he be good and hath attained Insight,
> He is a sage (*muni-*) that hath escaped the yoke (of earthly
> existence).'

Exactly to that effect was it spoken by the Blessed One, so I have heard.

§ 54. This verily was said by the Blessed One, said by the Sanctified One, so I have heard.

'There are these three Cravings (*esana-*), O monks.' 'What three?' 'The Craving for Lust, the Craving for Existence, and the Craving for a life of chastity (*brahmacariya-*).[2] These verily, O monks, are the three Cravings.'

To this effect spake the Blessed One, and hereupon said the following:

> 'The self-composed, mindful,
> And thoughtful disciple of Buddha,
> Comprehendeth the Cravings,
> And the cause of the Cravings,

---

[1] *vivattayi;* a caus. formation from root *vṛt-;* lit. 'turning apart, aside,' hence the idea of 'breaking.'

[2] This curious passage apparently is to be taken as showing that all sorts of ties, or clinging to earthly matters, whether good or bad, are wrong, and as proving that complete detachment from the world is the Buddhist goal.

And comprehendeth where they cease,
And the Path that leadeth to their destruction.
By the destruction of (his) Cravings,
This monk hath extinguished Hunger, and hath attained
   Nirvāna.'

Exactly to that effect was it spoken by the Blessed One, so I
have heard.

§ 55. This verily was said by the Blessed One, said by the
Sanctified One, so I have heard.

'There are these three Cravings, O monks.' 'What three?'
'The Craving for Lust, the Craving for Existence, and the Crav-
ing for a life of chastity. These verily, O monks, are the three
Cravings.'

To this effect spake the Blessed One, and hereupon said the
following:

   'The ascertainment of the truth that there is a Craving for
      Lust,
   A Craving for Existence, and a craving for the life of
      chastity—
   (The ascertainment of this truth, I say) cometh
   From a mass (*samussaya-*) of Subjects of Belief.[1]

   In the case of him that hath desisted from all Passion,
   Who is released from the destruction
   Caused by Thirst, the cravings are gotten rid of,
   And the subjects of belief are removed.
   By the destruction of (his) cravings
   A monk becometh devoid of hope (*nirāsa-*) and leaveth off
      inquiry.'[2]

Exactly to that effect was it spoken by the Blessed One, so I
have heard.

---

[1] *diṭṭhi-ṭṭhāna-*, Skt. *dṛṣṭi-sthāna-*, compounded with the following *samus-
saya-*.

[2] The first of the above stanzas shows how the deduction is gained from a
mass of speculation, while the second stanza shows that when one has gained
this knowledge, he rises by its aid, and no longer has any need of speculation.

§ 56. This verily was said by the Blessed One, said by the Sanctified One, so I have heard.

'There are these three Taints,[1] O monks.' 'What three?' 'The Taint of Lust, the Taint of Existence, and the Taint of Ignorance. These verily, O monks, are the three Taints.'

To this effect spake the Blessed One, and hereupon said the following:

> 'The self-composed, mindful,
> And thoughtful disciple of Buddha,
> Comprehendeth the Taints,
> And the cause of the Taints,
>
> And comprehendeth where they cease,
> And the Path that leadeth to their destruction.
> By the destruction of (his) Taints, he
> Hath extinguished Hunger, and hath attained Nirvāna.'

Exactly to that effect was it spoken by the Blessed One, so I have heard.

§ 57. This verily was said by the Blessed One, said by the Sanctified One, so I have heard.

'There are these three Taints, O monks.' 'What three?' 'The Taint of Lust, the Taint of Existence, and the Taint of Ignorance. These verily, O monks, are the three Taints.'[1]

To this effect spake the Blessed One, and hereupon said the following:

> 'He that hath destroyed the Taint
> Of Lust, and who hath abandoned
> Ignorance, and the Taint of Existence,
> And who is freed and without the Substrata—
> Such a one hath conquered Māra (*i. e.* the Tempter)
> With his elephant, and hath put on his final body.'

Exactly to that effect was it spoken by the Blessed One, so I have heard.

[1] See page 65, note 2.

§ 58. This verily was said by the Blessed One, said by the Sanctified One, so I have heard.

'There are these three Thirsts, O monks.' 'What three?' 'The Thirst for Lust, the Thirst for Existence, and the Thirst for Non-existence. These verily, O monks, are the three Thirsts.'

To this effect spake the Blessed One, and hereupon said the following:

'Those creatures that are joined
To the yoke of Thirst, with minds
Impassioned by Existence and Non-existence—
These men joined to the yoke of Māra,
And without Security (a-yogakkhema-) go to Transmigra-
tion,
To Birth and Death.

Whosoe'er abandon Thirst, (and are)
Without the Thirst for Existence or Non-existence—
They (while) in the world have passed over (to the other
shore) ;
They acquire the destruction of the Taints.'

Exactly to that effect was it spoken by the Blessed One, so I have heard.

§ 59. This verily was said by the Blessed One, said by the Sanctified One, so I have heard.

'A monk that is endowed with three things, O monks, hath escaped the realm of Māra, and shineth like the sun.' 'With what three (things)?' 'Here (in this world) a monk becometh endowed with the advanced Attribute (khanda-) of Character (sīla-), O monks, he becometh endowed with the advanced Attribute of Contemplation (samādhi-), he becometh endowed with the advanced Attribute of Wisdom (pañña-); when endowed with these three things, O monks, he hath passed beyond the realm of Māra, and shineth like the sun.'

To this effect spake the Blessed One, and hereupon said the following:

> ' He that is rightly inspired[1]
> In Character, Contemplation, and Wisdom,
> Hath passed beyond the realm of Māra,
> And shineth like the sun.'

Exactly to that effect was it spoken by the Blessed One, so I have heard.

[End of] First Chapter [of the third division]

Résumé 6

Source and Element (§§ 50, 51) ; then two (on) Feelings (§§ 52, 53) ;

And two (on) Cravings (§§ 54, 55) ; two (on) Taints (§§ 56, 57) ;

And from Thirst (§ 58)[2] ; then from the realm of Māra (§ 59).[2]

(These), they say, (form) the first, last, and highest chapter.[3]

§ 60. This verily was said by the Blessed One, said by the Sanctified One, so I have heard.

' There are, O monks, these three essentials (*vatthu-*) of virtuous deeds (*puñña-kiriya-*).' ' What three?' ' The essentials of virtuous deeds consisting of Charity (*dāna-*), Character (*sīla-*), and Devotion (*bhāvana-*). These verily, O monks, are the three essentials.'

To this effect spake the Blessed One, and hereupon said the following :

> ' One should learn virtue
> Which is of extensive goal, and (which hath)
> The faculty[4] of Happiness ;

---

[1] *su-bhāvitā;* lit. ' Character, Contemplation, and Wisdom—of whom these are well-inspired.'

[2] Both of these words are put in the abl. case metri gratia.

[3] It is to be noted that this résumé is the only one of the eleven in the book which is written in the *tristubh* meter, *i. e.* in lines of eleven syllables each.

[4] *indriya-;* consult Childers, *Pāli Dict.,* s. v., for the five ' faculties ' of happiness, misery, enjoyment, grief, and indifference. ' Faculty ' is the rendering

And one should devote oneself
To Charity, to tranquil behavior (*samacariya-*)
And to thoughts of Friendship.

Having devoted himself to these three virtues,
Which provide reason for happiness,
A wise man gaineth the world of Happiness—
A world all free from distress.'[1]

Exactly to that effect was it spoken by the Blessed One, so I have heard.

§ 61. This verily was said by the Blessed One, said by the Sanctified One, so I have heard.

'There are these three Eyes (*cakkhu-*), O monks.' 'What three?' 'The natural eye, the divine eye, and the eye of Wisdom. These are the three eyes, O monks.'

To this effect spake the Blessed One, and hereupon said the following:

'The natural eye, the divine eye,
The eye of Wisdom preeminently—
These three eyes
The Excellent One hath proclaimed.

The birth[145] of the natural eye
(Is) the path of the divine eye,
Inasmuch as knowledge was born[2]
As the eye of wisdom.
By the attainment of this eye
One is released from all Misery.'

adopted by Mrs. Rhys Davids, *DhS.* §§ 661, 709, 971 ; I follow that rendering here and in the identical stanzas in § 22, but elsewhere I have translated as 'sense.'

[1] This poetical section seems to have no direct connection with the prose portion above ; the same two stanzas occur also in § 22, where similarly they have no connection with the prose portion of the same section. As the two stanzas offer no especial difficulty to the translator, it may be assumed, I think, that both § 22, and this section, § 60, are either later additions to the text of the Iti-vuttaka, or else represent a rearrangement of the text.

[2] *uppāda-*, Skt. *ut-pad-*, 'to arise, to be born, to come into existence.'

Exactly to that effect was it spoken by the Blessed One, so I have heard.

§ 62. This verily was said by the Blessed One, said by the Sanctified One, so I have heard.

'There are these three senses,[1] O monks.' 'What three?' 'The sense (which says): "I shall know that which is not known"[2]; the sense of knowledge (aññā-); the sense of having thoroughly known.[3] These are the three senses, O monks.'

To this effect spake the Blessed One, and hereupon said the following:

'Of a novitiate-monk who is under religious training,[4]
Who is following the straight path—his first understanding (ñāṇa-)
Lieth in (the doctrine of) Destruction;
Therefore Knowledge (aññā-) is (his) neighbor.

Of such a one as is released by Knowledge (aññā-), therefore,
There is the Understanding (ñāṇa-):
"I have genuine (akuppa-) Emancipation
From the destruction caused by the Fetters of Existence."

That good man, verily, who is possessed of his senses,[5]
Who is delighted in the condition of Repose (santi-pada-),

---

[1] See page 71, note 4.

[2] I analyze this compound into anaññātaṃ, aññassāmi, iti, indriyaṃ.

[3] aññātāvindriyaṃ; the former part of this compound is aññāta- plus the suffix -āvin, for which see Whitney, Skt. Gram., § 1232. These three 'senses,' or 'faculties,' are evidently knowledge as to the future, the present, and the past. Incidentally compare the Buddhist order of words, differing from the usual English order of past, present, and future. Compare § 63, following.

[4] sikkhamana-, ppl. from root śikṣ-, from which comes also the word sekkha-, 'novitiate-monk,' in the line above.

[5] This passage is apparently in curious contrast to the narrower meaning of indriya-, 'organ of sense,' as exemplified in §§ 28, 29. The word is here taken evidently in the more philosophical meaning of 'faculty,' which are enumerated (see Mrs. Rhys Davids, DhS. § 971-3) as 'vision, hearing, smell, taste, body-sensibility, femininity, masculinity, and vitality.' At best the passage is somewhat unsatisfactory. We should expect rather: 'One who thoroughly comprehends the senses,' as in the Dīgha Nikāya, Pāli Text Soc. edition, sutta 22, as translated by Warren, Buddhism, p. 366.

Putteth on his final body, (for he)
Hath conquered Māra with his elephant.[1]

Exactly to that effect was it spoken by the Blessed One, so I
have heard.

§ 63. This verily was said by the Blessed One, said by the
Sanctified One, so I have heard.[2]

'There are these three times,[3] O monks.' 'What three?'
'Time which has passed, time which has not arrived (*i. e.*
future), and time which is present.[4] These are the three times,
O monks.'

To this effect spake the Blessed One, and hereupon said the
following:

'Creatures that believe in[5] the Indestructible,[6]

---

[1] *sa-vāhana-;* lit. 'with his vehicle.'

[2] It is with great diffidence that I attempt to translate this section, as I
have found it well-nigh impossible to glean any connected or intelligent sequence
from the following lines.

[3] *addha-;* I take this word to be equivalent to the Skt. *adhvan-,* 'road,
distance, time.' The writer of the above very brief prose introduction to this
section has not, I feel sure, himself fully understood the meaning of the following stanzas. The only possible connection to be discerned between the
prose and the poetry is precisely this rare and somewhat doubtful word *addha-.*
The only word in the stanzas to which this word can possibly refer is to
akkheyya, on which see my note below. Aside from this single problematical
rapport, there is not the slightest light thrown by this prose passage on the
stanzas which follow.

[4] For the characteristic order of past, future, and present see § 62 preceding, note 3, and compare § 78.

[5] *saññino;* I compare this with Skt. *sam-jñā-,* which Böhtlingk and Roth
define as 'glaubend an'

[6] *akkheyya-;* this word presents great difficulty. I have translated it as
if it were equivalent to Sanskrit *a-kṣeya-,* a guṇa formation from the root
kṣi-, 'to kill, to destroy.' Of this, however, I feel by no means sure. Another possibility is that the Pāli term may be equivalent to Skt. *ākhyā-* plus the
suffix *īya* (for this suffix cf. Whitney, *Skt. Gram.,* § 1215 a, b, where he cites
parvatīya, 'mountainous'); this Sanskrit word *ākhyā-* is itself extremely rare,
being cited only once in Böhtlingk and Roth ('Zeitdauer'). A plausible
argument for this rendering of the Pāli term is afforded by the occurrence
of *addha,* 'time,' in the prose above. Still a third possibility is that it may
equal Skt. *ākhyeya-,* 'what ought to be proclaimed,' from the root *khyā-,* 'to
tell.' Force is given to this third interpretation by the occurrence of the word
akkātāra-, 'teacher,' *i. e.* 'one who tells,' in line f.

That are established in (*paṭiṭṭhita-*) the Indestructible
Without Thorough Knowledge (*a-pariññā-*) of the Inde-
structible,
Go to the Bond of Death.

And by having Thorough Knowledge of the Indestructible,
(a person)
Doth not think of it as his leader (*akkhātāra*) (lit. teacher),
And by his mind (*manasā*) he hath attained
Release (*vimokkha-*), the incomparable condition of Repose.

This one, verily, possessed of the Indestructible,
Upright (*santa-*), being delighted by the Condition of
Repose,
Worshipping[1] wisely,[2] and abiding in the Law,
He is not accounted as a Veda-student.'[3]

Exactly to that effect was it spoken by the Blessed One, so I
have heard.

§ 64. This verily was said by the Blessed One, said by the
Sanctified One, so I have heard.

'There are these three evil actions (*duccarita-*), O monks.'
'What three?' 'The evil actions of the body, word, and
thought.[4] These are the three evil actions, O monks.'

To this effect spake the Blessed One, and hereupon said the
following:

'He that hath committed
Any evil action of body,
Word, or thought, or any other action

___

[1] *sevi-;* lit. 'following, serving.'

[2] *saṅkhāya;* I take this as an abl. case of Skt. *saṃkhyā-*, 'enumeration,
reckoning, calculation; a number, numeral; reason, understanding, intellect;
deliberation, reflection.' Childers cites this adverbial usage.

[3] The last verse of the Pāli reads: *saṅkham nopeti vedagū*, lit. 'he does
not come into account as a Veda student'—probably a blow at the brahmans.

[4] *manas-;* here, and in similar passage enumerating this threefold division
of good or evil acts, I have rendered *manas-* as 'thought,' owing to the
common English phrase 'deed, word, and thought,' but have in other places
translated the same word *manas-* as 'mind.'

Called a crime; or who
Hath not done any good action,
But hath done much evil—
After the dissolution of the body
This unwise one goeth to perdition.'

Exactly to that effect was it spoken by the Blessed One, so I have heard.

§ 65. This verily was said by the Blessed One, said by the Sanctified One, so I have heard.

'There are these three good actions, O monks.' 'What three?' 'The good actions of body, word, and thought. These are the three good actions, O monks.'

To this effect spake the Blessed One, and hereupon said the following:

'He that hath abandoned
Evil actions of body,
Word, and thought, and all other actions
Called criminal; and who

Hath not done any improper action,
But hath done much that is proper—
After the dissolution of the body
This wise one goeth to heaven.'

Exactly to that effect was it spoken by the Blessed One, so I have heard.

§ 66. This verily was said by the Blessed One, said by the Sanctified One, so I have heard.

'There are these three purifications,[1] O monks.' 'What three?' 'The purifications of body, word, and thought. These are the three purifications, O monks.'

To this effect spake the Blessed One, and hereupon said the following:

'He that is pure in body, word, and thought (*cetas-*),
And free from taint,[2] possessed of

---

[1] *socceyya-*, Skt. *sauca-*, plus suffix *-iya*, see Whitney, *Skt. Gram.*, § 1216.
[2] See page 65, note 2.

Purity and purification—
He, they say, hath abandoned all.'

Exactly to that effect was it spoken by the Blessed One, so I have heard.

§ 67. This verily was said by the Blessed One, said by the Sanctified One, so I have heard.

'There are these three silences,[1] O monks.' 'What three?' 'The silences of body, word, and thought. These are the three silences, O monks.'

To this effect spake the Blessed One, and hereupon said the following :

'He that is silent in body, word, and thought (*manas-*),
Free from taint, (and) possessed of
The quality of silence of a Muni (*muni-moneyya-*)—
He, they say, hath washed away[2] his sin.'

Exactly to that effect was it spoken by the Blessed One, so I have heard.

§ 68. This verily was said by the Blessed One, said by the Sanctified One, so I have heard.

'Whoso, O monks, hath not abandoned Passion, Hate, and Delusion[3]—he is called Māra's bond, Māra's snare for the unliberated one,[4] and one that must act according to the will of a sinful man.

'Whoso, O monks, hath abandoned Passion, Hate, and Delusion—he is not called Māra's bond, (he is not called) Māra's snare for the liberated one,[5] or one that must act according to the will of a sinful man.'

---

[1] *moneyya-*, Skt. *mauna-*, 'taciturnity.' The word is connected with the term *muni*, 'an ascetic, a sage,' whose great duty is silence.

[2] *ninhāta-;* I derive this word from *nis-*, or *niḥ-*, plus the root *snā-*, 'to bathe, wash.' This particular compound form is not found in Sanskrit. I assume a modification of the first sibilant, as *sn* in Skt. regularly corresponds to *ṇh* in Pāli.

[3] *moha-*, glossing *avijjā-*, 'ignorance,' in verse b below.

[4] *patimukkassa*, contrasted with *oramukkassa*, 'liberated,' below.

[5] Observe the curious litotes: 'the liberated one hath no snare of Māra.'

To this effect spake the Blessed One, and hereupon said the following:

' He that hath renounced Passion, Hate, and Ignorance—
This man, they say, is one whose soul is increased,
One that hath become a Brahma, a Consummate One,
A Buddha, having passed beyond enmity and fear, and having
  abandoned all.'

Exactly to that effect was it spoken by the Blessed One, so I have heard.

§ 69. This verily was said by the Blessed One, said by the Sanctified One, so I have heard.

' That monk or nun,[1] that hath not abandoned Passion, Hate, and Delusion, O monks, is said not to have crossed the Ocean, with its waves and its billows, with its whirlpools, sharks,[2] and demons (*rakkhasa-*). But whatsoever monk hath abandoned Passion, Hate, and Delusion, is said to have crossed the Ocean with its waves and its billows, with its whirlpools, sharks, and demons, and when he hath crossed over and gone to the other shore, he standeth on the dry land of Brahma.'

To this effect spake the Blessed One, and hereupon said the following:

' He that hath renounced Passion, Hate and Ignorance,
Hath crossed o'er the Ocean,
With its sharks and its demons, with its danger from waves,
And (which is) difficult of crossing.

He that hath got rid of the Substrata and abandoned Death,
That hath escaped Misery through not being born again—
He, when dead (lit. gone home), goeth not to similar (Exist-
  ence)—
Him I call a king of Death (*maccu-rāja-*), (gone) beyond
  Delusion.'

---

[1] *bhikkhunī-;* the only time that a nun is mentioned in this work. The only other feminine touch is in § 42 preceding.

[2] *gaha-*, Skt. *graha-*. In Skt. the same word has also the meaning ' croco-dile.' Compare a similar passage in § 109.

[End of] Second Chapter [*i. e.* of the third division]

Résumé 7

Virtue (§ 60); the eye (§ 61)[1]; then the sens(es) (§ 62)[2]; "Times" (§ 63); two on action (§§ 64, 65)[3]; pure (§ 66)[4]; Silen(ces) (§ 67)[5]; then two on Passion (§§ 68, 69).[6]

These, moreover, they say, (form) the highest (*uttama-*) second chapter.[7]

§ 70. This verily was said by the Blessed One, said by the Sanctified One, so I have heard.

'Those creatures seen by me, O monks, who are attended by evil actions of body, word, or thought, who speak ill of the noble ones, holding Wrong Belief,[8] taking on themselves the deeds of Wrong Belief—such persons, after the dissolution of the body after death, go to punishment, misfortune, torture, and perdition.

'Now, not having heard this (truth) proclaimed by anyone else, whether devotee or brahman, I say: "Those creatures seen by me, O monks, who are attended by evil actions of body, word, and thought, who speak ill of the noble ones, holding Wrong Belief, taking on themselves the deeds of Wrong Belief— such persons, after the dissolution of the body after death, go to punishment, misfortune, torture, and perdition."

'And furthermore, since this is entirely[9] understood, seen, and known, for that reason I say: "Those creatures seen by me, O monks, who are attended by evil actions of body, word, and

---

[1] Observe the stem form.

[2] In order to keep within the eight syllables of the verse, the last word of this line of the résumé is apocopated into *indriyā-*, instead of *indriyāni* of the text. This shortened form may be, however, comparable to the Vedic plural, see Whitney, *Skt. Gram.*, § 331 c, and cf. Fausböll, Sutta Nipāta, *SBE.* 10, p. xii.

[3] Remark the singular *caritam*, instead of the plural *caritāni*.

[4] Remark the simple adj. instead of the abstract *soceyya-* of the text.

[5] *mune* instead of *moneyyāni* of the text.

[6] All MSS. agree in having the stem form *rāga-* instead of the nom. *rago*.

[7] The fourth line of this résumé has four extra syllables.

[8] *diṭṭhi-*; see note on § 49.

[9] *sama-*; an unusual word. Probably equivalent to Avestan *hāma-*; cf. Bartholomae, *Altiranisches Wörterbuch*, s. v.

thought, who speak ill of the noble ones, holding Wrong Belief, taking on themselves the deeds of Wrong Belief—such persons, after the dissolution of the body after death, go to punishment, misfortune, torture, and perdition." '

To this effect spake the Blessed One, and hereupon said the following:

> ' That individual here (in this world)
> Who reflecteth wrong thoughts,[1]
> Who uttereth wrong words,
> Who doeth wrong deeds with his body,
>
> Who is ignorant and wicked
> Here in this brief life—(he),
> After the dissolution of the body,
> Goeth to perdition.'

Exactly to that effect was it spoken by the Blessed One, so I have heard.

§ 71. This verily was said by the Blessed One, said by the Sanctified One, so I have heard.

' Those creatures seen by me, O monks, who are attended by good actions of body, word, and thought, who speak no ill of the noble ones, holding Right Belief, taking on themselves the deeds of Right Belief—such persons, after the dissolution of the body after death, go to felicity and heaven.

' Now, not having heard this (truth) proclaimed by anyone else, whether devotee or brahman, I say: " Those creatures seen by me, O monks, who are attended by good actions of body, word, and thought, who speak no ill of the noble ones, holding Right Belief, taking on themselves the deeds of Right Belief— such persons, after the dissolution of the body after death, go to felicity and heaven."

' And furthermore, since this is entirely understood, seen, and known, for that reason, I say: " Those creatures seen by me, O monks, who are attended by good actions of body, word, and thought, who speak no ill of the noble ones, holding Right Belief,

---

[1] Literally *manas-*, ' mind.'

taking on themselves the deeds of Right Belief—such persons, after the dissolution of the body after death, go to felicity and heaven." '

To this effect spake the Blessed One, and hereupon said the following :

> ' That individual here (in this world)
> Who reflecteth right thoughts,
> Who uttereth right words,
> Who doeth right acts with his body,
>
> Who is learned and virtuous
> Here in this brief life—(he),
> After the dissolution of the body,
> Goeth to heaven.'

Exactly to that effect was it spoken by the Blessed One, so I have heard.

§ 72. This verily was said by the Blessed One, said by the Sanctified One, so I have heard.

' There are, O monks, these three Elements (*dhātu-*) of Deliverance (*nissarana-*).' ' What three?' ' Deliverance from the Passions, namely, Separation (*nekkhamma-*) (*i. e.* from the world); the Deliverance from Form (*rūpa-*), namely Formlessness; the Deliverance from that which has had Existence, which is compounded (and) subject to the Chain of Causation (*paticca-samuppanna-*), namely, Cessation (*nirodha-*).'

To this effect spake the Blessed One, and hereupon said the following:

> ' The ever-fervent one that knoweth
> The Deliverance from Passion,
> And (the way of) passing beyond Forms,
> And attaineth tranquillity of all the Aggregates—
>
> This monk, verily, hath proper vision (*sammaddasa-*),
> Inasmuch as he is emaciated here (in this world) ;
> If he be good and hath attained Insight,

7

He verily is a sage (*muni-*) that hath escaped the yoke (of earthly existence).'

Exactly to that effect was it spoken by the Blessed One, so I have heard.

§ 73. This verily was said by the Blessed One, said by the Sanctified One, so I have heard.

'Those (people) that are (liberated) from Form, O monks, are better than (people still attached to) Form; Cessation is (even) better than (the state of individuals who are attached to) Form.'

To this effect spake the Blessed One, and hereupon said the following:

' Those creatures that go to Form (*rūpa-upa-gam-*),
And those that live without Form,
Do not comprehend Cessation,
Since they go to Re-existence.

And those, who, by their comprehension of Forms,
Are not stablished in formless things,
(And) who are emancipated through Cessation—
These persons have abandoned death.

He that hath attained with his body
The immortal Element (*dhātu-*) of getting-rid-of-the-Sub-
strata (*nirūpadhi-*),
And who, free from Taint,[1]
Hath experienced the getting-rid-of-the-Substrata—
He, a Perfectly Enlightened One, pointeth out the Path
Which is without grief and free from passion.'

Exactly to that effect was it spoken by the Blessed One, so I have heard.

§ 74. This verily was said by the Blessed One, said by the Sanctified One, so I have heard.

' There are these three (kinds of) sons, O monks, to be found

---

[1] See page 65, note 2.

living in the world.' 'What three?' 'Superior-born, equal-born, and inferior-born.[1]

'In what way, O monks, doth a son become superior-born? There exist here (in this world), O monks, parents who have not gone to the Refuge of the Buddha, who have not gone to the Refuge of the Law, who have not gone to the Refuge of the Order, who do not abstain[2] from maltreating living creatures, who do not abstain from not giving gifts,[3] who do not abstain from fornication,[4] who do not abstain from falsehood, who do not abstain from the state of sloth (characteristic) of a drinker of liquor and spirits, who are immoral; of them there is born a son that goeth to the Refuge of the Buddha, that goeth to the Refuge of the Law, that goeth to the Refuge of the Order, who abstaineth from maltreating living creatures, who abstaineth from not giving gifts, who abstaineth from fornication, who abstaineth from falsehood, who abstaineth from the state of sloth (characteristic) of a drinker of liquor and spirits, who is moral and righteous: thus, verily, O monks, is born a superior son.

'In what way, O monks, doth a son become equal-born? There exist parents here (in this world), O monks, who have gone to the Refuge of the Buddha, who have gone to the Refuge of the Law, who have gone to the Refuge of the Order, who abstain from maltreating living creatures, who abstain from not giving gifts, who abstain from fornication, who abstain from falsehood, who abstain from the state of sloth (characteristic) of a drinker of liquor and spirits, who are moral and righteous; of them there is born a son that goeth to the Refuge of the Buddha, that goeth to the Refuge of the Law, that goeth to the Refuge of the Order, who abstaineth from maltreating living creatures, who abstaineth from not giving gifts, who abstaineth from fornication, who abstaineth from falsehood, who abstaineth

[1] *ati-, anu-, ava-jāta-*.
[2] *atipāta-;* see Monier Williams, *Sanskrit Dictionary,* s. v.
[3] Notice the double negative instead of the positive.
[4] Literally, 'wrong conduct in love affairs.'

from the state of sloth (characteristic) of a drinker of liquor and spirits, who is moral and righteous: thus, verily, O monks, is born an equal son.

' In what way, O monks, doth a son become inferior-born. There exist parents here (in this world), O monks, who have gone to the Refuge of the Buddha, who have gone to the Refuge of the Law, who have gone to the Refuge of the Order, who abstain from maltreating living creatures, who abstain from not giving gifts, who abstain from fornication, who abstain from falsehood, who abstain from the state of sloth (characteristic) of a drinker of liquor and spirits, who are moral and righteous; of them there is born a son that doth not go to the Refuge of the Buddha, that doth not go to the Refuge of the Law, that doth not go to the Refuge of the Order, who doth not abstain from maltreating living creatures, who doth abstain from giving gifts, who doth not abstain from fornication, who doth not abstain from the state of sloth (characteristic) of a drinker of liquor and spirits, who is immoral and wicked: this, verily, O monks, is born an inferior son. These are the three (kinds of) sons, O monks, to be found living in the world.'

To this effect spake the Blessed One, and hereupon said the following:

' The wise desire a son superior
    Or equal; they desire not
    An inferior-born son
    Who injureth the family.

Those sons who in the world become
    Followers (of Buddha), who are endowed
    With a faithful character, bountiful,[1] unselfish—
    May the moon, detached from the mass of clouds, shine
      upon them.'

Exactly to that effect was it spoken by the Blessed One, so I have heard.

[1] *vadaññū-*, Skt. *vadānya-*.

§ 75. This verily was said by the Blessed One, said by the Sanctified One, so I have heard.

'There are found these three (kinds of) individuals living in the world, O monks.' 'What three?' 'One that is like unto a lack of rain, one that giveth rain over a district, and one that giveth rain everywhere. How doth an individual, O monks, become like unto a lack of rain? An individual here becometh not a giver of all things, namely, (the articles) food, drink, clothing, conveyance, garlands, perfumes, unguents, bed, lodging, and light, to devotees, brahmans, beggars, wayfarers, and indigent people—thus, forsooth, O monks, an individual becometh like unto a lack of rain.

'How doth an individual, O monks, become like unto one that giveth rain over a district? An individual here becometh a giver of certain things, but of certain other things he becometh not a giver, namely, (the articles) food, drink, clothing, conveyance, garlands, perfumes, unguents, bed, lodging and light, to devotees, brahmans, beggars, wayfarers and indigent people—thus, forsooth, O monks, an individual becometh like unto one that giveth rain over a district.

'How doth an individual, O monks, become like unto one that giveth rain everywhere? An individual here giveth[1] of all things, namely, (the articles), food, drink, clothing, conveyance, garlands, perfumes, unguents, bed, lodging, and light, to devotees, brahmans, beggars, wayfarers, and indigent people—thus, forsooth, O monks, an individual becometh like unto one that giveth rain over a district.

'These verily, O monks, are the three (kinds of) individuals found living in the world.'

To this effect spake the Blessed One, and hereupon said the following:

---

[1] Observe the changed locution. Above in this same passage, it was the noun *dātā-*, 'a giver'; here it is the verb *deti*, 'to give.' The latter may correspond to the Skt. root *day-*, 'to share,' or to the root 1 *dā-*, 'to give,' or possibly to 2 *dā-*, 'to divide, to share.' There are no MS. variants.

' He (that) distributeth not
That which he hath received—
His food, his drink, his sustenance—
Unto devotee, brahman, beggar, wayfarer—
Such a low man as he, they say, is like
Unto a lack of rain.

He that is giver of certain things,
Of certain giving not—[1]
Such as he, so say the wise,
Sheddeth rain over a district.

A man that doth promise[2] plenteous alms,
Compassionate to all creatures,
Scattereth wide (his bounty) with joy and pride,[3]
And saith: " Share, share[4] (with me)."

Like unto a cloud that roareth,
And thundereth,
And giveth forth rain,
And filleth the heights and the depths
With its drenching waters—
Such here on earth is that man.[5]

When he hath toilfully[6] acquired
Wealth—attained by lawful means—
He satisfieth with food and drink
The worthy (*sammā*) wayfarers.

Exactly to that effect was it spoken by the Blessed One, so I
have heard.

---

[1] *pavecchati;* a rare word equiv. to Skt. *pra-r̥-,* or *r̥ch-,* ' to go forth,' in
the caus. ' to send, to give.'   For the euphonic *v* before *i, e, u,* see Franke,
Pāli und Sanskrit, p. 101.

[2] *subhikkhavāca-,* lit. ' with assurance of good provisions.'

[3] Remark that *māna-* may in Pāli, as in Sanskrit, be used in a good, as
well as in a bad, sense.

[4] *detha;* an imper. 2d pl., from either 1 *dā-,* ' to give,' or from 2 *dā-,* ' to
divide, to share.'

[5] Rather an anticlimax !

[6] *utthāna-,* Skt. *ut-sthāna-,* lit. ' rising.' In Apte, *Skt. Dict.,* s. v., the
fourth definition is ' effort, exertion.'

§ 76. This verily was said by the Blessed One, said by the Sanctified One, so I have heard.

'A man should preserve his character (*sīla-*), O monks, by seeking three (kinds of) Happiness.' 'What three?' 'He should preserve his character by thinking: "Let praise come to me"; he should preserve his character by thinking: "Let wealth fall to my lot"; he should preserve his character by thinking: "I shall go after the dissolution of the body after death, to felicity, to the heavenly world (*sagga-loka-*)." A wise man should preserve his character, O monks, by seeking these three (kinds of) Happiness.'

To this effect spake the Blessed One, and hereupon said the following:

'A wise man may preserve his character
If he seek three (kinds of) Happiness, namely,
Praise, the getting of treasure,
And, when dead, joy in heaven.

But if, though not doing evil himself,
He attendeth on one that doth evil,
He becometh suspected[1] of evil,[2]
And his ill-repute increaseth.

As is the friend whom one maketh,
As is the friend on whom one attendeth,
Such a one doth he himself become.
Of such is the nature of Association (*sahavāsa-*).

As the poisoned shaft besmeareth the unsmirched quiver,
Just so one comrade (influenceth) another comrade,
And the toucher the touched.
Thus from fear of being smirched
A steadfast man should not be
An evil man's companion.

---

[1] *samkiya-;* not in Childers. I should compare the word with Skt. *śaṅk-*, 'to doubt; to imagine, fancy.'

[2] For this use of the loc. case see Speyer, *Sanskrit Syntax*, p. 109.

Like unto a man that wrappeth up
A stinking fish in Kusa¹ grass,
And the grass giveth forth a stinking savor—
Like unto him are those that attend on fools (*bālu-*).

And like unto a man that wrappeth
A (morsel of the fragrant) Tagara² within a petal,³
And the leaves give forth a pleasant savor—
Like unto him are those that attend the steadfast.

Hence if he know the contents⁴
Of his own leaf-basket,⁵
The wise man should not serve the wicked,
But should serve the good,
For the wicked lead (one) to perdition,
But the good cause (one) to attain felicity.'

Exactly to that effect was it spoken by the Blessed One, so I have heard.

§ 77. This verily was said by the Blessed One, said by the Sanctified One, so I have heard.

'That this body is undergoing decomposition, O monks, is the Law of the change of Intellections⁶; that all the Substrata are transitory (and cause) misery, is the Law of Transformation.'

To this effect spake the Blessed One, and hereupon said the following:

---

¹ *Poa cynosuroides*, a sacred grass used at certain religious ceremonies.

² *Tabernae montana coronaria*, a fragrant plant.

³ *Patāsa-;* we should expect *patta-,* 'leaf,' to be used a second time.

⁴ I follow the MSS. B, D, E, and S in reading *sampāka*. This means literally 'cooking, or ripening thoroughly' (Monier Williams). The word also designates a plant, *viz.,* the *Cathartocarpus Fistula.*

⁵ *palāsa-puta-;* this may be a reference to the *piṭakas*, or 'baskets,' of tradition, the well-known designation of the three divisions of the Buddhist canon.

⁶ *viññāna-;* this word is discussed by Mrs. Rhys Davids, *DhS.* §§ 16, 202, 484, 1008, 1156.

'Knowing both (the fact) that the body
    Is undergoing decomposition, and that the Intellections
      are breaking up,[1]
(The man) of perfected mind, that hath seen peril in
    the Substrata,
And learned[2] Birth and Death—
He hath attained unto the highest Repose,
And longeth for his time to come.'[3]

Exactly to that effect was it spoken by the Blessed One, so I have heard.

§ 78. This verily was said by the Blessed One, said by the Sanctified One, so I have heard.

'This is a fundamental principle, O monks, that creatures mingle and unite together with creatures, the base-disposed with the base-disposed, and the well-disposed with the well-disposed.

'In past time it was a fundamental principle that creatures have mingled and united together with creatures, the base-disposed with the base-disposed, and the well-disposed with the well-disposed.

'In future time it will be a fundamental principle that creatures will mingle and unite together with creatures, the base-disposed with the base-disposed, and the well-disposed with the well-disposed.

'At the present time it is now a fundamental principle that creatures do mingle and unite with creatures, the base-disposed with the base-disposed, and the well-disposed with the well-disposed.'[4]

To this effect spake the Blessed One, and hereupon said the following:

[1] The best MS., namely M, it may be noted, reads *verāgunam*, which is not clear to me. I follow the MSS. D, E, and S in reading *pabhaṅguṇam*.

[2] *ajjhagā;* an aor. of *adhi-gam-*, used as an aor. of *adhīte*, 'to repeat, to go over,' hence 'to study.'

[3] *kāla-*, a synonym of death.

[4] For the Buddhistic order of 'past, future, and present,' see note on § 62 and cf. § 63.

'The undergrowth[1] of the forest (of Lust) is born from
  Contact (*samsagga-*)
And perisheth from lack of Association.
Just as one that hath climbed upon a small[2] piece of wood,
Would sink in the great sea,
So doth even the man of holy life sink
When he approacheth an indolent person.

Therefore, forsaking the indolent person
With enfeebled strength,
Let one live with wise men
Who are in retreat (and) noble,
With minds intent, meditative,
Ever undertaking manly deeds.'

Exactly to that effect was it spoken by the Blessed One, so I
have heard.

§ 79. This verily was said by the Blessed One, said by the
Sanctified One, so I have heard.

'These three things, O monks, conduce to the deterioration of
a monk who is a novitiate.' 'What three?' 'A monk becometh
here (in this world) delighting in and delighted by activity,[3]
O monks, and addicted to the delight of activity; he becometh
delighting in and delighted by conversation and addicted to the
delight of conversation; he becometh delighting in and delighted
by sleep, and addicted to the delight of sleep. These, O monks,
are the three things which conduce to the deterioration of a
monk who is a novitiate.

'These three things, O monks, conduce to the non-deterioration
of a monk who is a novitiate.' 'What three?' 'A monk becometh not here (in this world) delighting in and delighted by

---

[1] *vanatha-;* literally the word means 'forest-standing,' and hence 'undergrowth.' In Skt. the term is used to designate 'hermit, ascetic.' For the use
of this word in the category of 'Lust,' see Mrs. Rhys Davids, *DhS.* § 1059.
See Dhammapāda, vv. 283, 284, 344.

[2] *paritta-;* Skt. *pari-dā-,* for which see Pāṇini, 5. 3. 124. In Sanskrit this
rare word has the meaning 'to circumscribe, to limit.'

[3] *kamma-;* there is here manifestly no idea of the Karma doctrine.

activity and becometh not addicted to the delight of activity;
he becometh not delighting in and delighted by conversation,
and becometh not addicted to the delight of conversation; he
becometh not delighting in and delighted by sleep, and becometh
not addicted to the delight of sleep. These, O monks, are the
three things which conduce to the non-deterioration of a monk
who is a novitiate.'

To this effect spake the Blessed One, and hereupon said the
following:

> ' Such a monk as delighteth in activity—
> As is delighted by conversation—and delighteth
> In sleep, and is puffed up (*uddhata-*),
> Cannot attain Supreme Enlightenment.
>
> Therefore, verily, one should be
> With few obligations,
> With slight slumber, and not puffed up;
> Such a monk can attain Supreme Enlightenment.'

Exactly to that effect was it spoken by the Blessed One, so I
have heard.

[End of the] Third Chapter [*i. e.* of the third division]

Résumé 8

Two on Belief (§§ 70, 71)[1]; Deliverance (§ 72); Form
(§ 73)[2];

A " son " (§ 74)[2]; and by " one that doth not give rain "
(§ 75);

---

[1] The writer of the résumé has totally misunderstood this passage. He
should not have written *diṭṭhi-*, 'Belief,' but *diṭṭhā* a passive past ppl. of *dṛś-*,
'to see.' The important word, at any rate, is not this verb 'to see,' but the
term *kāyaduccarita-* in the same line of the text. Compare the résumé of
§ 81, found after § 89 in this translation. This section begins in just the same
way as §§ 70, 71, but in this latter résumé the important word *sakkārena*, 'own
affairs,' is correctly given. It is, however, to be noted that this difference may
have been caused by the metrical position of the respective words in the verses
of the two résumés.

[2] In the former case the sing. instead of the plur. is used, in the latter
case the plur. is used instead of the sing.

Happi(nesses) (§ 76)[1]; and Dissolution (§ 77); and Element (§ 78);

By Deterioration (§ 79)[1]; these ten.

§ 80. This verily was said by the Blessed One, said by the Sanctified One, so I have heard.

' There are, O monks, these three improper Ideas.'

' What three?' ' The improper Idea attached to Consideration,[2] the improper Idea attached to gain (lābha-), to one's own affairs (sakkāra-), and reputation (siloka-), the improper Idea attached to lack of compassion for another.[3] These verily, O monks, are the three improper Ideas.'

To this effect spake the Blessed One, and hereupon said the following:

' He that is attached to consideration,
    To gain, to one's own affairs, and esteem,
    That taketh pleasure in companionship—
He is far from the destruction of the Fetters.

But (lit. and) he that hath abandoned children and herds,
    Dwelling apart and abandoning society—[4]
Such a monk as this is able
    To attain Supreme Enlightenment.'

Exactly to that effect was it spoken by the Blessed One, so I have heard.

---

[1] For the apocopated form, cf. the preceding résumé, page 79, note 2.

[2] vitakka-; this word is rendered ' Conception ' by Mrs. Rhys Davids, DhS. §§ 7, 160, 167, a rendering which, though suitable to a work of the psychological character of the Dhamma Sanghani, would not be as appropriate here.

[3] anavaññatti-; this unusual word is not in Childers. I should compare it with the Skt. *an-ava-jñāpti-. From the Skt. verb jñā-, ' to know,' is formed the noun jñāpti-, ' knowledge,' although the verb ava-jñā-, ' to despise, to contemn,' does not have in Sanskrit a corresponding noun *ava-jñāpti-; it is to this hypothetical form with a negative prefix an-, that I compare this Pāli word.

[4] anuddayatā-; this seems to be a genuine Pāli word. See Samyutta-Nikāya, edited by Leon Feer, vol. 2, p. 218, and also the Vinaya Pitaka, edited by Windisch, vol. 2, p. 196. Compare also Mrs. Rhys Davids, DhS. § 1056. Childers, Pāli Dict., s. v., correlates the word with Skt. anudayā-, ' pity.'

[5] sangha-, apparently not used here in the usual acceptation of ' the Order.'

§81. 'I have seen creatures, O monks, who were overcome, whose thoughts were taken possession of by their own affairs (*sakkāra-*). who, after the dissolution of the body after death, go to punishment, misfortune, torture, and perdition. Those creatures seen by me, O monks, who are overcome, whose thoughts are not taken possession of by their own affairs, after the dissolution of the body after death, go to punishment, misfortune, torture, and perdition. Those creatures seen by me, O monks, who are overcome, whose thoughts neither are nor are not taken possession of by their own affairs, after the dissolution of the body after death, go to punishment, misfortune, torture, and perdition.

'Now, not having heard this (truth) of (*i. e.* promulgated by) anyone else, whether devotee or brahman, I say: "Those creatures seen by me, O monks, who are overcome, whose thoughts are taken possession of by their own affairs, after the dissolution of the body after death, go to punishment, misfortune, torture, and perdition. Those creatures seen by me, O monks, who are overcome, whose thoughts are not taken possession of by their own affairs, after the dissolution of the body after death, go to punishment, misfortune, torture, and perdition. Those creatures seen by me, O monks, who are overcome, whose thoughts neither are nor are not taken possession of by their own affairs, after the dissolution of the body after death, go to punishment, misfortune, torture, and perdition."

'And furthermore since this entirety is understood, seen, and known by me, for that reason I say: "Those creatures seen by me O monks, who are overcome, whose thoughts are taken possession of by their own affairs, after the dissolution of the body after death, go to punishment, misfortune, torture, and perdition. Those creatures seen by me, O monks, who are overcome, whose thoughts are not taken possession of by their own affairs, after the dissolution of the body after death, go to punishment, misfortune, torture, and perdition. Those creatures seen by me, O monks, who are overcome, whose thoughts neither are nor are not taken possession of by their own affairs, after the dissolution of the body after death, go to punishment, misfortune, torture, and perdition." '

> ' He whose Contemplation (*samādhi-*)
> Neither is nor is not disturbed
> By his own affairs
> And that liveth attentively—

> Him, thoughtful, persevering, (and) discerning the subtle
> (*sukhuma-*) Belief,
> Whose delight is in the destruction
> Of the Clinging to Existence (*upādāna-*)—
> Him they call a good man.'

§ 82. ' These three divine reports, O monks, go forth time after time[1] among the gods.' ' What three?' ' At the time, O monks, when a holy disciple hath cut off his hair and beard, and hath donned the yellow robes, (when he) aimeth at the houseless life (of an ascetic) by his renunciation of home—at this time, O monks, the divine report goeth forth among the gods: " This holy disciple aimeth at fighting with the devil (*Māra*)." This, O monks, is the first divine report which goeth forth among the gods time after time.

' And furthermore, at the time, O monks, when a holy disciple liveth (joined with the junction of Devotion, *i. e.*) devoted to the seven laws accessory to Supreme Enlightenment—at this time, O monks, the divine report goeth forth among the gods: " This holy disciple fighteth with the devil." This O monks, is the second divine report which goeth forth among the gods time after time.

' And furthermore, at the time, O monks, when a holy disciple liveth, having by the destruction of the Taints known fact to face and attained in (this) seen world Emancipation of thought and Emancipation of wisdom—at this time, O monks, the report goeth forth among the gods: " This holy disciple is victor

---

[1] Edmunds, *Buddhist and Christian Gospels*, p. 145, translates the phrase *samayā samayaṃ upādāya*, as ' from time to time.' The words appear to mean literally ' time including time.'

in the conflict, (and) since he hath conquered (at) the battle-front, he dwelleth beyond.[1] This, O monks, is the third divine report which goeth forth among the gods time after time. These verily, O monks, are the three divine reports which go forth among the gods time after time.'

> ' Even the gods verily will do homage unto him
> Whom they have seen to be victor in the conflict,
> A disciple of Supreme Enlightenment,
> Great, time-surpassing.

> " Homage unto thee, O unconquerable one!
> Thou who hast overcome the hard to conquer,
> Who hast constantly overcome
> The army of Death by Release (*vimokkha-*)."

> Thus will the gods do homage unto him
> That hath attained the goal (*mānasa-,* lit. purpose) ;
> They will do homage unto him
> Because he proceedeth[2] to the power over Death.'

§ 83. ' O monks, when a god hath fallen from Dharma in his body, there appear five prognostics: garlands wither, garments become soiled, sweat is emitted from the armpits, a bad color cometh upon his body, the god taketh no pleasure in his divine ambrosia.

' The (other) gods, O monks, when they have learned that this son of a god hath fallen from Dharma, sympathize with him in three phrases, namely, " Go hence, sir, unto felicity (*sugati-*), and when thou hast gone thither, do thou take that which is good to take (*suladdha-lābham labha*), and when thou hast so done, do thou be firmly established therein." '[3]

When this was said a certain monk spake unto the Blessed One in this manner: ' What in sooth, Sire, is considered an attainment of felicity on the part of the gods, and what, Sire, a

---

1 *ajjhāvasati,* Skt. **adhy-ā-vas-;* this would seem to imply ' he dwelleth in Nirvāna.'

2 *vajati,* Skt. root *vraj-*.

3 *suppatiṭṭhita-,* Skt. *su-prati-sthā-*.

taking of what is good to take on the part of the gods, and further, Sire, what is considered " being firmly established therein " on the part of the gods?' 'Humanity (*manussatta-*) verily, O monks, is considered an attainment of felicity on the part of the gods. The Faith which a devotee, when he hath become human, doth acquire from the discipline of the law made known by the Consummate One—this (Faith) verily, O monks, is considered on the part of the gods a taking of what is good to take. Furthermore this Faith becometh fixed in him (lit. of him) firmly established (because) born from the depths of his being, firm, not to be restricted by devotee, or brahman, or god, or devil, or by brahman or anyone else in the world; this verily, O monks, is considered on the part of the gods " being firmly established therein." '

> ' When, owing to the uncertainty of life,
> A god falleth from his divine body
> Three reports go forth among the gods
> In sympathy with him :—

> " Go hence, sir, unto felicity,
> Unto companionship[1] of men,
> And, when thou hast become human,
> (Go unto) the unsurpassed Faith.

> " This is the Faith of thee (who art) fixed therein[2]
> A Faith that is born from the depths (of thy being),
> Not to be shaken[3] as long as life doth last;
> It is made known[4] in the True Law.

[1] *sahavyataṃ;* I take this as the acc. sing. of a nom. *sahavyatā,* and compare it with Skt. **saha-vya-tā-.* In Sanskrit the suffix *-vya* is not common as a secondary suffix (see Whitney, *Skt. Gram.,* § 1228 c), and seems to be used exclusively with words expressing relationship, *e. g., pitṛvya-,* 'paternal uncle.' The suffix *-vya* is exemplified in Pāli in other words, *e. g., dāsavyaṃ-,* 'servitude, slavery,' and *paṭavyatā-,* Skt. *pātavyatā-,* 'injury, slaying.'

    nivittha-, Skt. *ni-vṛtta-,* from the root *vṛt-,* 'to turn.'

[3] *asaṃhīrā;* I take this word as a formation from *sam-īrati,* comparing it with the Skt. *īr-,* 'to set in motion, to shake.' For the insertion of the letter *h* see Pischel, *Grammatik der Prakrit-Sprachen,* § 338. It must be noted, however, that *samīrati* without the *h* does not occur in Pāli. Franke, *Pāli und Sanskrit,* p. 101, n. 63, says: 'Vortritt von *h* nicht überall belegt.'

[4] *suppavedite;* compare Skt. causative of *su-pra-vid-.*

" For, having avoided
　　Evil actions of body,
　　Word, and thought,
　　That hath evil repute,[1]

" And having done much and boundless good
　　In body, word, and thought,
　　One doth become
　　Freed from the Substrata.

" For by giving he hath acquired this great virtue
　　Which is related to the Substrata;
　　Verily he hath stablished other mortals
　　According to the True Law of Chastity."

When the gods know that a god hath fallen,
　　With this kindly feeling[2]
　　They do encourage him—
" Be thou a god again and again." '

§ 84. ' There are these three individuals, O monks,[3] who are born into the world for the advantage and for the felicity of many persons, out of kindly feeling for the world, for the benefit, for the advantage and for the felicity of gods and men.' ' What three?' ' Here in the world, O monks, is born the Sanctified One, the Supremely Enlightened One, who is endowed with knowledge and (good) behavior, who is felicitous, who knoweth the world, an unsurpassed guider of men that have to be tamed, a teacher of gods and men, enlightened, blessed. He it is that expoundeth the law of the beginning, middle, and end of good acts, and who maketh known the Teacher with his characteristics, (and who maketh known) the full and perfect life of Chastity. This, O

---

[1] *dosa-saññita-*, Skt. *dosa-sam* $=$ *jñā-*.

[2] *imāya kampāya;* in form this may be either an instr., dat., abl., or gen. It is probably an instr. of quality, equivalent to the Latin abl. of quality. See Speyer, *Sanskrit Syntax,* p. 50, para. 3.

[3] The vocative occurs only in S.

8

monks, is the first individual that is born into the world for the advantage and for the felicity of many persons, out of kindly feeling for the world, for the benefit, for the advantage, and for the felicity of gods and men.

'And moreover, after him, O monks, there is (an individual) who is called a disciple of the Teacher, sanctified, with Taints destroyed, who doeth his duty, who hath laid aside his burden, who hath attained the right goal (*attha-*), with Bonds of Existence completely destroyed, emancipated by perfect knowledge. He it is that expoundeth the law of the beginning, middle, and end of good acts, and who maketh known the Teacher with his characteristics, (and who maketh known) the full and perfect life of Chastity. This verily, O monks, is the second individual that is born into the world for the advantage and for the felicity of many persons, out of kindly feeling for the world, for the benefit, for the advantage, and for the felicity of gods and men.

'And moreover, after him, O monks, there is (an individual) who is called a disciple of the Teacher, a novitiate imbued with intelligence,[1] learned, endowed with that which maketh for Character (*sīlavat-*). He it is that expoundeth the law of the beginning, middle, and end of good acts, and who maketh known the Teacher with his characteristics, (and who maketh known) the full and perfect life of Chastity. This, O monks, is the third individual that is born into the world for the advantage and for the felicity of many persons, out of kindly feeling for the world, for the benefit, for the advantage, and for the felicity of gods and men. These verily, O monks, are the three individuals who are born into the world for the advantage and for the felicity of gods and men.'

' The Teacher verily is the first great Sage in the world;
Following him is the disciple of perfected mind,
And then next the novitiate, imbued with intelligence,
Learned, endowed with that which maketh for Character.

---

[1] *pātipada-*, a *vrddhi* derivative of Skt. *prati-pad-*.

These three, teachers of gods and men,
Givers of radiance, speaking forth the Law,
Unclose the door of immortality[1];
They release many from the Bond.

Those who, by the unsurpassed leadership of the Teacher,
Follow on the path which hath well been shown,
And those who are earnest in the teachings of the Felicitous One,
Make an end of Misery e'en here (in the world).'

§ 85. 'Ye should live, O monks, seeing what is impurity in the body; there should likewise be present before you internally attention (lit. memory) to your inhalation and exhalation (*ānāpāna-*); ye should live seeing impermanence in the Aggregates.

'And of those that live seeing what is impurity in the body, whatever inclination (*anusaya-*) toward Passion there is (in them), (all that inclination) is destroyed by their elements of purity (lit. by their pure element).

'And (likewise) from having present before oneself internally attention to (one's) inhalation and exhalation, whatever external repositories of ideas (*i. e.* modes of thought) there are, which tend toward hindrance, they become of no account (lit. do not exist).

'And of those that live seeing the impermanence which is in the Aggregates—whatever ignorance there is in those people, (all that ignorance) is destroyed, and whatsoever sapience (*vijjā-*) there is in those people, (all that sapience) cometh to the fore.'[2]

'The one that seeth what is impure in the body,
With his thoughts fixed on inhalation and exhalation,
Seeing the tranquillity (*samatha-*) of all the Aggregates,
Ardent at all times,

---

[1] This phrase is in absolute contradiction with the usual Buddhist doctrine, which states distinctly that immortality is not and should not be the goal of the righteous man.

[2] *uppajjati,* lit. 'rises up, comes into being.'

This monk verily hath proper vision
Inasmuch as he is emancipated here (in this world) ;
If he is good and hath attained Insight, ·
He is a sage that hath escaped the yoke of earthly existence.'

§ 86. 'This is a lesser law unto a monk that hath entered upon his greater and his lesser laws. In explanation[1] of the phrase "that hath entered upon his greater and his lesser laws": he is one that speaketh that which is lawful, he is one that speaketh not that which is unlawful; he is one that reflecteth on that which is lawful, he is one that reflecteth not on that which is not lawful. When he hath accomplished[2] both of these things, he liveth resigned,[3] thoughtful, and mindful.'

'The monk that delighteth in and is delighted by the Law,
That doth meditate upon the Law,
That remembereth the Law,
Doth not abandon the True Law.

If in going or in standing,
Or in sitting or in reclining,
He gaineth supremacy over[4] his own thoughts,
Truly that one goeth to Repose.'

§ 87. 'There are these three improper ideas, O monks, which cause blindness, lack of sight, and ignorance, bring about cessation of wisdom, tend toward hindrance, and conduce to absence of Nirvāna.' 'What three?' 'The idea of Lust, O monks,

[1] *veyyakaranāya*, cf. Skt. *vyākarana-*, 'Auseinandersetzung.' I am indebted to the kindness of Dr. Truman Michelson for the explanation of this form as a dative of purpose. See Kuhn, *Pāli Grammatik*, 70. The word is not cited in Childers with this meaning.

[2] *abhinivajjetvā*; this may be analyzed as a gerund of *abhi-ni-varjayati*, from the root *vrj-*. The compound does not appear in Sanskrit. Consult Böhtlingk and Roth under *abhivarga-*, defined as 'Bereich.'

[3] The foregoing prose passage very strongly confirms, it seems to me, the view advanced in the Introduction, p. 9–10, namely, that the prose portions of the Iti-vuttaka are in the nature of a commentary. This particular one does not seem to have a very close connection with the following stanzas.

[4] *samayam*; I take this as a pres. participle of the root *śam-*.

causeth blindness, lack of sight, and ignorance, bringeth about cessation of wisdom, tendeth toward hindrance, and conduceth to absence of Nirvāna. The idea of Malevolence, O monks, causeth blindness, lack of sight, and ignorance, bringeth about cessation of wisdom, tendeth toward hindrance, and conduceth to absence of Nirvāna. The idea of Cruelty, O monks, causeth blindness, lack of sight, and ignorance, bringeth about cessation of wisdom, tendeth toward hindrance, and conduceth to absence of Nirvāna.[1]

'There are these three proper ideas, O monks, which do not cause blindness, lack of sight, and ignorance, which do not bring about cessation of wisdom, which tend not toward hindrance, (but) which conduce to Nirvāna.' 'What three?' 'The idea of Separation (*nekkhamma-*), O monks, causeth not blindness, lack of sight, and ignorance, doth not bring about cessation of wisdom, doth not tend toward hindrance, (but) conduceth to Nirvāna. The idea of Non-malevolence, O monks, causeth not blindness, lack of sight, and ignorance, doth not bring about cessation of wisdom, doth not tend toward hindrance, (but) conduceth to Nirvāna. The idea of Non-cruelty, O monks, causeth not blindness, lack of sight, and ignorance, doth not bring about cessation of wisdom, doth not tend toward hindrance, (but) conduceth to Nirvāna.'

'One should reflect on the three proper ideas, and should renounce
The three improper ones. He verily that doth reflect upon
And doth subdue[2] his ideas, as the rain doth subdue
Dust that is raised—he truly e'en here (in this world)
By gaining supremacy over his ideas by his thought (or, heart),
Hath gone unto a condition of Repose.'

§ 88. 'There are, O monks, these three internal impurities, internal foes, internal enemies, internal murderers, and internal

---

[1] Compare the similar passage in § 110.
[2] Literally ' subdues his reflected-ou ideas.'

adversaries.' 'What three?' 'Desire, O monks, is an internal impurity, foe, enemy, murderer, and adversary. Hate, O monks, is an internal impurity, foe, enemy, murderer, and adversary. Delusion, O monks, is an internal impurity, foe, enemy, murderer, and adversary. These verily, O monks, are the three internal impurities, foes, enemies, murderers, and adversaries.'

' Desire begetteth unseemliness (*anattha-*) ;
Desire exciteth the thoughts ;
A person is not aware of this danger
Which is born from within.

The man that is dominated by Desire
Doth not know what is seemly and seeth not the Law ;
That man whom Desire doth accompany,
Becometh like unto murky (*andha-*) darkness.

And he that hath abandoned Desire,
And desireth not the things that make for Desire—
From him Desire doth pass away
As doth a drop of water from the lotus.

Hate begetteth unseemliness ;
Hate exciteth the thoughts ;
A person is not aware of this danger
Which is born from within.

The man that is dominated by Anger
Doth not know what is seemly and seeth not the Law ;
That man whom Hate doth accompany,
Becometh like unto murky darkness.

And he that hath abandoned Hate,
And hateth not the things that make for Hate—
From him Hate doth pass away
As doth Tāl[1] fruit from its stem.

---

[1] From this word comes the English term ' toddy '; see *Hobson-Jobson,* s. v. With this Pāli word compare the Hindustani *tāṛi,* ' the fermented sap of the *palmyra.*'

Delusion begetteth unseemliness;
Delusion exciteth the thoughts;
A person is not aware of this danger
Which is born from within.

The man that is under Delusion
Doth not know what is seemly and seeth not the Law;
That man whom Delusion doth accompany
Becometh like unto murky darkness.

And he that hath abandoned Delusion, and is not deluded
By the things which make for Delusion—
He doth dispel all Delusion,
As the rising sun (dispelleth) the darkness.'

§ 89. This verily was said by the Blessed One, said by the
Sanctified One, so I have heard.

'By three[1] errors, O monks, was Devadatta overcome and overpowered in spirit (lit. 'thought'), and was (caused to) stay for
an aeon of time in punishment and perdition without relief.'[2]
'By what three?' 'By sinful longing, O monks, was Devadatta
overcome and overpowered in spirit, and caused to stay for an
aeon of time in punishment and perdition without relief. By
sinful association, O monks, was Devadatta overcome and overpowered in spirit, and caused to stay for an aeon of time in
punishment and perdition. But when, in truth, he became mindful of his higher duties,[3] he did enter, by means of his mundane
conduct[4] and his attainment of discrimination, upon[5] the (fitting)
end. By these three errors verily, O monks, was Devadatta
overcome and overpowered in spirit, and caused to stay for an
aeon of time in punishment and perdition.'

---

[1] There seems to be something missing from the text, as only two 'errors'
are mentioned in this prose passage, as far as I understand it.

[2] *atekiccha-*, from the verb *tikicchati*, Skt. *cikitsati*, 'to treat medically, to
cure.'

[3] A locative absolute.

[4] *oramattaka-*, not clear to me (possibly compare Skt. *avara-* and *marta-?*).

[5] *antarā āpādi*, literally 'entered within.'

To this effect spake the Blessed One, and hereupon said the following:

'Let no one be born in any world soever
Having sinful longings;
Know ye this also by this[1] (my message)
(Namely) how is the road of them that have evil longings.

I have heard that Devadatta,
Who was termed " wise,"
And who was considered to be " of perfected mind,"
Was resplendent in glory.

But having acted carelessly[2]
And offended[3] the Consummate One,
He reached the Waveless perdition[4]
Four-portaled and frightful.

For whosoever harmeth[5] an inoffensive[6] man
That hath done no deed of evil,
Upon him indeed (*i. e.* the offender), being offensive in
    thought
And lacking in respect, evil will light.[7]

Whoso should think to pollute
The ocean by a jar of poison,
He could not pollute it by that,
For the sea is great(er) than the jar.

---

[1] *tadaminā* is the reading of all the texts, except B, which reads *tadāminā*, and S, which has *tadiminā*. I follow the latter reading, and analyze the word into *tad-*, 'this,' and *iminā-*, an instrumental case of one of the stems of the demonstrative pronoun *ayam*. See Whitney, *Skt. Gram.*, § 501.

[2] Literally ' having walked after carelessness.'

[3] *āpajja;* I take this to be a gerund of *ā-pad-*. See Apte, *Skt. Dict.*, under the third meaning, ' to get into misfortune, fall into trouble.'

[4] One of the eight *narakas*, or hells, regarded as the most dreadful.

[5] *dubbhe*, an opt. 3rd sing., Skt. *druhyet*. See Kuhn, *Pāli Grammatik*, p. 42.

[6] *aduttha-*, probably analogous to Skt. *a-duh-stha-*.

[7] It seems to me that the causative *phusseti*, Skt. *spṛś-*, is out of place here, and I should therefore follow B in reading *phussati*.

Even so he that (thinketh to) injure by a word
The Consummate One;
A word doth not reach unto Him,
Walking uprightly, good in thought.

A wise man should make such a one his friend,
And should follow him,
In following whose path,
A monk may attain destruction of Misery.'

Exactly to that effect was it spoken by the Blessed One, so I
have heard.

[End of the] Fourth Chapter [*i. e.* of the third division]

Résumé 9

Idea (§ 80)[1]; his own affairs (§ 81)[1]; report (§ 82)[1];
Falling (§ 83)[2]; in the world (§ 84); offensive (§ 85);
Law (§ 86)[3]; causing blindness, (§ 87)[4]; impurity (§ 88);
By Devadatta (§ 89)[5]; these ten.

§ 90. This verily was said by the Blessed One, said by the
Sanctified One, so I have heard.

'There are, O monks, these three kinds of Serenity[6] in the Highest.' 'What three?' 'As many creatures as there are, O monks,
whether without feet, or with two feet, or with four feet, or with
many feet, or having form, or without form, sentient or non-
sentient, or neither sentient nor non-sentient—highest above them
all is accounted the Consummate One, the Sanctified One, the

---

[1] Note the stem forms, *vitakka-, sakkāra-, sadda-,* instead of the nom. case.

[2] Note the participle *cavamāna-* instead of the noun *cavana-*.

[3] We should expect *anudhammo,* 'Lesser Law,' as is in the text.

[4] In the text of this section the important word is *akusala-vitakka-,* 'improper ideas,' and is modified by a list of adjectives. The writer of this
résumé has simply chosen the first one of this list in place of the important
noun which it modifies

[5] Note the use of the instrumental case for the sake of the meter.

[6] *agga-pasāda-,* Skt. *agra-prasāda-;* the second element in Skt. means
'condescension, propitiousness, serenity, calmness.' The word *agga-* is found
no less than eleven times in the stanzas below.

Perfectly Enlightened One. Whatsoever (persons), O monks, have found Serenity in the Highest, they have found Serenity in that which is Highest, and unto them, moreover, that have found Serenity in the Highest, there cometh highest fruition.

As many laws as there are, O monks, whether compounded or not compounded, the highest of them is accounted absence of passion, that is to say, the effacing of lasciviousness, the repression of thirst (*pipāsa-*), giving up one's abode, refraining from conversation[1], destruction of Thirst (*taṅha-*); (for) absence of passion (is) Cessation, Nirvāna.

'Whatsoever (persons), O monks, have found Serenity in the law of the absence of passion, they have found Serenity in that which is Highest, and unto them, moreover, that have found Serenity in the Highest, there cometh highest fruition.

'Whatsoever perfected laws there are, O monks, the noble eightfold Path is proclaimed to be the soul (*ātman-*) of them. For example: Right Belief, right resolves, right words, right occupations (*kammanta-*), right ways of living, right exertion, right reflection, right Contemplation (*samādhi-*).

'Whatsoever (persons), O monks, have found Serenity in the law of the Noble Faith, they have found Serenity in that which is Highest, and to them that have found Serenity in the Highest, there cometh highest fruition.[2]

'Whatsoever Orders or Congregations there are, O monks, the highest of these is accounted the Order of the disciples of the Consummate One, namely, four couples of men, eight individuals[3], this is the Order of the disciples of the Blessed One, (this Order) worthy of worship, worthy of hospitable treatment, worthy of offerings, worthy of salutation, the unsurpassed realm (lit. field) of virtue in the world.[4]

'Whatsoever persons, O monks, have found Serenity in the

[1] *vattum*, infin. of *vatti*, Skt. *vac-*.

[2] The two preceding paragraphs are found only in S.

[3] One is tempted to take this small number of members in the Congregation, or Order, as an indication of the beginnings of the Buddhist monasteries, and as perhaps implying an early date of compilation of this work.

[4] The preceding paragraph is not in S.

Order, they have found Serenity in that which is Highest, and to
them that have found Serenity in the Highest, there cometh highest fruition.'

To this effect spake the Blessed One, and hereupon said the
following:

> ' Of them that have found Serenity in that which is highest,
>   Comprehending the Highest Law,
>   Having found Serenity in the Highest Buddha,
>   Worthy of offerings (and) unsurpassed—
>
> Of them that have found Serenity in the Highest Law
>   Which stilleth Lusts and is happy (*i. e.* giveth happiness)
>   Having found Serenity in the Highest Order,
>   The unsurpassed realm of virtue—
>
> Of those giving gifts of the first fruits—
>   (Of all these) the highest virtue increaseth,
>   And likewise the highest life and repute,[1]
>   Fame, renown, happiness, (and) power.
>
> The wise one that is a giver of that which is highest,
>   Who is intent on the Highest Law,
>   Whether he be god or mortal,
>   He doth rejoice in his attainment of the Highest Goal.'

§ 91. 'This, O monks, is the lowest of vocations, namely, the
(vocation of) a Piṇḍola; this word,[2] O monks, refers to the fact
that Piṇḍola wandered about in the world with bowl in hand.
And there come unto[3] this very man, O monks, the sons of
(noble) family, (sons who) are possessed of[4] wealth, for

---

[1] *vanna-*, Skt. *varṇa-*, primarily ' color, beauty,' then ' caste.'   It can hardly
have the latter meaning here, as the Buddhistic tendency was away from caste.

[2] *abhilāpa-*, lit. ' the designation (is derived from) the fact that (*iti*).'

[3] *vasika-;* this word can mean either ' under the control, or possession, of '
and ' empty, devoid of.'

[4] From this point throughout the remainder of this section, I confess
extreme uncertainty in my interpretation. The only facts of which I feel
fairly sure are that Piṇḍola at first had a good reputation and attracted noble

the sake of[1] the possession of wealth; not only those that are brought before kings are[2] made religious mendicants, nor those brought before robbers, nor yet those in debt, nor those in fear(?). And furthermore (there come)[3] those who are o'erspread with Misery, who are overcome with Misery, on account of birth, old age, death, griefs, lamentations, miseries, woes, and distresses, with the idea (*iti*) that possibly (*api eva nāma*) a termination of all this Aggregate of Misery may be learned from him that hath crossed beyond (birth, old age, etc.).

'And even so, O monks, this son of noble family (meaning Piṇḍola ?) becometh[4] covetous, with keen passion for Lusts, malevolent in thought, corrupt in his mind's aims, of forgetful memory, unmindful, not self-composed, with wandering thoughts, with untamed senses.

'Just as[5] a funeral torch, O monks, standing in a dung heap, giving light between both (*i. e.* the village and the forest ?), neither kindleth the store of faggots in the village, nor in the forest; by such a simile do I speak of this individual, (for) he hath, on the one hand, abstained from the enjoyments of the householder, and yet, on the other hand, he maketh not full the wealth of the order of devotees (?).'

'Having, on the one hand, abstained from the pleasures of the
    householder,
Yet, on the other, (being) ill-fortuned, with ruined self-respect
    (*māna-*, lit. pride),
He doth scatter forth the wealth of the order of the devotees;
He perisheth like a funeral torch.

followers, but later fell from grace, and after his fall is compared to the futile dying flame of a funeral torch. Are we to compare with this the story of Pindola-Bhāradvāja and the sandal bowl? See Kern, *Manual of Indian Buddhism* (Strassburg, 1896), pp. 32, 108.

[1] *paticca*, Skt. *pratītya*, lit. 'going up to, for the purpose of.'
[2] I follow S in omitting *na* before *ājīvikā pakatā*.
[3] Supplying *upenti* from the preceding sentence.
[4] Omit *so ca*, following B, C, M, P, Pa, S.
[5] On *seyyathā* compare page 126, note 2.

Better would it be to swallow a heated iron **ball,**
Like flaming fire, than that a bad,
Unrestrained fellow should live
On the charity of the land.'

§ 92. 'Even if a monk should gather up the edges of his robe
and follow behind me,[1] and should walk in my footsteps (lit.
step by step), yet if he should become covetous,[2] with keen
passion for Lusts, malevolent in thought, corrupt in the aspiration of his mind, of heedless memory,[3] unmindful, not self-
composed, letting his thoughts wander, with his senses unculti-
vated,[4] then is he far from me and I from him.' 'Why?'
'Because, O monks, that monk seeth not the Law, and seeing
not the Law he seeth not me.

'But if a monk should dwell even a hundred leagues from me[5]
and be not covetous, nor with keen passion for Lusts, nor malevolent in thought, nor corrupt in his mind's aspiration, (but) heedful in memory, mindful, self-composed, noble in thought, with
his senses cultivated, then is he near to me and I to him.'
'Why?' 'Because, O monks, that monk seeth the Law, and
seeing the Law, he seeth me.'

---

[1] *pitthito anubandho;* the former word is analogous to Skt. *prsthatas,* 'from
the rear, behind.' The latter word *anubandha-* is, in my opinion, a wrong
reading; it is glossed in Böhtlingk and Roth as 'Band, Verbindung, ununter-
brochene Reihe oder Folge; Absicht.' The compound verb *anu-bandhati,* however, means 'to follow.' I should therefore change the reading in the Pāli
to *anubaddho,* a past participle of this verb. Edmunds, who has translated
the prose portion of this section, *Buddhist and Christian Gospels,* p. 149, has
the same translation as above.

[2] *abhijjhālū,* Skt. *abhi-dhyā-,* 'longing, wish, desire,' plus the suffix *-ālū,*
for which compare Whitney, *Skt. Gram.,* § 1192 b and § 1227 b.

[3] *muttha-sati-;* for an explanation of the first member of this compound I
am indebted to my friend Mr. Chas. J. Ogden, who suggested that this word is
to be compared to the Skt. root *mrs-.* The past participle of this root does not
actually occur in any Sanskrit text, but this Pāli *muttha-* corresponds perfectly
to this hypothetical form in Sanskrit. Compare Pischel, *Grammatik der
Prakrit-Sprachen,* § 51.

[4] *pākata-;* this word corresponds to Skt. *prākrta-,* from which comes the
designation 'Prākrit' for the vulgar dialects.

[5] I follow the variant *me* instead of *so,* as it seems the better reading.

' If even a follower should become cupidinous and destructive,
See how far is the one that goeth after temptation,[1]

From him that goeth not after it;
How far is the one that is not content,
From him that is content;
How far the greedy one is from him that is devoid of greed.

And he that hath insight into the Law,
And is wise through his knowledge of the Law,
He, like a pool sheltered from the wind,[2]
Or like one without temptation, is absorbed in Repose.[3]

See how near he that is without temptation
Is to him that is without temptation;
How near he that is tranquil is to him that is tranquil;
How near he that is unselfish is to him that is unselfish.'

§ 93. ' There are these three Fires, O monks.'   ' What three?'
' The Fire of Passion, the Fire of Hate, the Fire of Delusion.
These verily, O monks, are the three fires.'

' The fire of Passion burneth mortals
Addicted to Lusts (and) stupefied;
The fire of Hate, moreover, burneth
The malevolent men, who kill living beings.

The fire of Delusion burneth the infatuated,
Those unskilled in the Noble Law;
These fires (consume) ignorant mankind
That take delight in their own bodies.

---

[1] *ejānuga-;* I analyze as *ejā-anuga-.*   The former word Mrs. Rhys Davids,
DhS. § 1059, translates as 'seduction.'   In the commentary of Buddhaghosa
to the Dhammapāda it is glossed by *ākaḍḍhana-,* ' drawing, attraction.'

[2] I follow S. reading *vūpasammati.*   Compare Childers, *Pāli Dict.,* under
vūpasamana-.

[3] I follow P, reading *rahado upanivāto va,* which to me is the only intelligible reading.   The extra syllable may be accounted for either by assuming
that the anaptyctic vowel of *rahado* does not count in the meter, or by assuming
synizesis with the following word.

They (*i. e.* the ignorant) swell (the realm of) perdition,
And the wombs of animals,
And the realm of the gods and the departed spirits (*pretas*),
Since they are not freed from the bonds of Māra.

And they that are devoted night and day
To the commandments of the Supremely Enlightened One—
Such people distinguish the fire of Passion
By being constantly aware of impurity.

Superior men, moreover, extinguish
The fire of Hate by friendship,
And the fire of Delusion by wisdom,
That wisdom which causeth one to attain Discrimination.

Those prudent (*nipaka-*) people having unweariedly
Night and day extinguished (these fires),
Attain Nirvāna absolutely,
And absolutely transcend Misery.

They, of noble vision, versed in the Veda,
Wise through right knowledge,
(And) having insight into the destruction of Birth,
Do not attain Re-existence.'

§ 94. 'A monk should so investigate, O monks, that when he hath[1] investigated externally (*bahiddhā*), his Intellection[2] becometh clear; since he doth not fear the future, through his not being attached to (what is) undiffused, internal, (and) non-static, he becometh possessed of no cause for the origin of the misery of Birth, Old Age, and Death.'

'A monk that hath abandoned the company of creatures,
That hath cut (loose from) the current,[3]
He hath utterly destroyed the Transmigration of Births;
He hath no Re-existence.'

---

[1] The *ca* here is difficult to explain.
[2] *viññāna-;* see page 88, note 6, with ref. there given.
[3] Compare the compound *āhāra-netti-*, 'current of subsistence,' in § 43.

§ 95. 'There are, O monks, these three sources[1] of Lust.'
'What three?' '(The sources are in) people that have Lust
for present things; (in people) that delight in created Lusts;
(in people) that are subject to Lusts created by others. These
verily, O monks, are the three sources of Lust.'[2]

> 'Those gods with Lust for present things,
>   Being subject to them . . .
> And those other gods who feast on Lust,
>   Delighting in created pleasures . . .[3]

> Under these and other circumstances
> A wise man should give up
> All Lust for sensual enjoyments
> Both divine and human.

> Cutting off the torrent hard to cross,
>   Which is connected with[4] what is pleasant and joyful,
> They attain Nirvāna absolutely;
> They absolutely transcend Misery.

---

[1] *upapatti-*, no Sanskrit cognate. It may be a formation from the compound **upa-pad-*. Childers, *Pāli Dict.*, s. v., defines as 'sensual existence' and cites three kinds of *kāma-upapattis*; they are (1) mankind and the four lowest *deva-lokas*, 'god-worlds', (2) *nimmana-rati*, 'created delight,' (3) *paranimmita-rati*, 'subjection to (Lusts) created by others.' I do not feel at all certain about the word.

[2] The brevity of this, as well as of the two preceding prose passages, is noteworthy. The prose in this particular passage is inadequate, it seems to me, for the purpose of an introduction and a commentary upon the stanzas which follow. It contains no reference to the last three stanzas, and, as I think, the explanation of the first stanza is not adequate.

[3] In my opinion something has been lost after the first stanza. The two *ye*'s ought to have two corresponding *te*'s. It must be said, however, that *vasavattino* and *nimmānaratino* might each be taken as a predicate in an eliptical clause, thus: 'What gods are with Lust for present things, (they are) subject to them; and what other gods are feasting on Lust, (they are) delighting in created things.' But the pronoun *ya-* usually has a correlative expressed, and for this reason I assume a break in the text after verse 4. As strengthening this view, it may be noted that there does not seem to be any grammatical connection between the first and second stanzas. Further evidence of textual corruption within this section lies in the fact that lines k-p are found word for word in § 93 preceding.

[4] *gadh-;* see page 48, note 3.

> They, of noble vision, versed in the Veda,
> Wise through right knowledge,
> (And) having insight into the destruction of Birth,
> Do not attain Re-existence.'

§ 96. 'He that is joined to the yoke of Lust, O monks, that is joined to the yoke of Existence, turning back, returneth to this world. He that is loosed from the yoke of Lust, O monks, (but) is joined to the yoke of Existence, doth not turn back or return to this world. He that is loosed from the yoke of Lust, O monks, and is loosed from the yoke of Existence, becometh a Sanctified One and hath his Taints destroyed.'

> 'Those creatures that are joined
> Both to the yoke of Lust
> And the yoke of Existence, go to Transmigration,
> And to Birth and Death.

> And those that have abandoned Lusts,
> But have not attained destruction of the Taints,
> (Even though still) joined to the yoke of Existence—
> They are called "Non-returners."

> And those that have ceased from Transmigration,[1]
> Destroying Re-birth, and who have attained
> Destruction of the Taints—they verily have in this world
> Crossed to the other shore.'

Third portion for recital

§ 97. 'A monk who is good in character, O monks, good in the Law, and good in Wisdom, is called "perfected in the discipline of the Law," he is (also) called a "Supreme Man." And how, O monks, doth a monk become good in Character? A monk becometh good in character here (in this world), O monks, (if) he liveth restrained by the restraint of the Precepts,[2] endowed

---

[1] I follow P, which reads *khina-saṃsārā*, as *-saṃsayā*, 'doubts,' does not seem so appropriate to the context.

[2] *pātimokkha-*; this is the name of an epitome, or brief list of rules, which precedes the Vinaya Piṭaka, the second of the three 'baskets' of the Buddhistic canon. For a good discussion, see Pavolini, *Buddhismo* (Milan, 1898), p. 79.

9

with a (wide) range of good behavior,[1] if he seeth danger in the
smallest faults, and if, having taken them upon himself, he doth
exercise himself in the Subjects of Study (*sikkāpāda-*).   Thus
verily, O monks, doth a monk become good in Character.   In
such manner is one good in character.

   'And how doth one become good in the Law?   A monk becometh good in the Law here (in this world), O monks, (if) he
liveth joined by the ties of Devotion to (lit. of) the things accessory to Enlightenment.   Thus verily, O monks, doth a monk
become good in the Law.   In such manner is one good in Character and good in the Law.

   'And how doth one become good in Wisdom?   A monk becometh good in Wisdom here (in this world), O monks, (if) he
liveth having even in the world, by the destruction of his Taints,
(gained) insight into the taintless Emancipation of Thought and
Wisdom, (and hath) himself known and seen them face to face.[1]
Thus verily, O monks, a monk doth become good in Wisdom.
In such manner, when one hath been called good in Character,
good in the Law, good in Wisdom, (and) perfected in the Discipline, he is called a "Supreme Man."'

'He that hath done no evil deed
   In body, word, or thought—
Him they call a "modest monk,"
(For they think:)   "He is good in Character."

He that is well-practised in the Laws,
Who goeth to the attainment of Enlightenment—
Him they call a "faithful (*anussada-*) monk,"
(For they think:)   "He is good in the Law."

---

   [1] *gocara-*, lit. 'cow-pasture,' then 'scope, range.'   Compare the Skt. compound *gocara-gata-*, 'having come within range of,' and *locana-gocara-*,
'within the range of vision.'
   [2] *sayam abhiññāya sacchikatvā upasampajja;* for a discussion of this phrase
see Childers, *Pāli Dict.*, p. 5, second column, at the bottom of the page.

He that himself understandeth the destruction
Of Misery here (in this world)—
Him they call a "taintless monk,"
(For they think:) "He is good in Wisdom."

He that is endowed with these Laws,
Who is free from wickedness, and hath cut loose from all
doubt,
Who is detached from all the world—
Him they call "forsaking all the world!"''

§ 98. 'There are, O monks, these two (kinds of) gifts, namely, material (*āmisa*-, lit. fleshly) and spiritual (*dhamma*-) gifts, and of these two, O monks, the higher is the latter.

'There are these two (kinds of) distributions, O monks, namely, material and spiritual distribution (*samvibhāga*-), and of these two, O monks, the higher is the latter.

'There are these two forms of kindliness (*anuggaha*-, lit. favor), namely, material and spiritual kindliness, and of these two the higher is the latter.'

'Since (men) have called the highest, unsurpassed gift,
That which the Blessed One hath described as distribution,
(Therefore) no wise, understanding person, whose tranquil
thoughts (are fixed) on the Chief Possession (*i. e.* Dharma),
Would offer sacrifice at (any) time.

And whatsoever persons both speak and hear (this doctrine),
With their tranquil thoughts (fixed) on the Commandment of
the Auspicious One,
And who are zealous in the Commandment of the Auspicious
One—
Their highest aim is purified.'

§ 99. This verily was said by the Blessed One, said by the Sanctified One, so I have heard.

'By means of the Law, O monks, do I account to be a brahman him that hath threefold knowledge, and no one else that merely talketh talk.[1] And how, O monks, do I account to be a brahman him that hath threefold knowledge, and no one else that merely talketh talk? Here (in this world), O monks, a monk doth recollect his former abode (*i. e.* his previous existence) variously appointed, thus[2]: "For one, two, three, four, five, ten, twenty, thirty, forty, fifty, a hundred, a thousand, a hundred-thousand births (*jāti-*), for several Saṃvat aeons, for several Revolution aeons, for several Saṃvat and Revolution aeons together, was I (born) there, with such and such a name, family, caste, means of subsistence, experiencing such and such good fortune and misfortune, and (living) such and such a span (*pariyanta-*) of life. When I departed thence,[3] I was (born) over there (*i. e.* in some other sphere of existence), with such and such a name, family, caste, means of subsistence, experiencing such and such good fortune and misfortune, and (living) such and such a span of life. When I departed from over there (*i. e.* the second sphere) I came into existence here." Thus doth he recollect his former abode (*i. e.* previous existence), variously appointed, with its shapes (*ākāra-*) and its regions. This, O monks, is the first knowledge attained by him; ignorance is destroyed and knowledge ariseth; darkness is destroyed and light

---

[1] *lapita-lāpana-mattena;* this word is taken without any change from the first stanza below, line 4. As this stanza is in the ordinary *śloka* metre, there is one syllable too many in this verse. I suggest that the verse below be emended to read *lapita-lāpana-mattam,* an emendation which not only satisfies metrical requirements, but in addition makes the passage an intelligible one, since the compound can now be construed as modifying the accusative *aṇṇaṃ,* 'some one else,' in verse 3, whereas the compound as it stands is in the instrumental case, and so, I think, impossible of explanation.

The fact that the writer of the prose portion of this section did not appreciate the defective meter, and was not troubled by the curious use of the instrumental case, seems, I think, to strengthen my argument that he often did not wholly and completely understand the verses himself.

[2] On *seyyathā* compare page 126, note 2.

[3] In spite of all the MSS. I have ventured to omit *amutra udapādiṃ,* 'came into being there,' as the two words seem to be pleonastic with the following *tatrapāsiṃ,* 'I was born there'; the latter I change into *tatrāsiṃ,* a possible emendation of the variant in C, *tatrāsi,* thus paralleling the preceding *amutrāsiṃ.*

ariseth, since he doth live ardent and resolute in mind, not disregarding Him.[1]

'And furthermore, O monks, by his divine vision (lit. eye), which is pure and transcending what is human, a monk doth see creatures that have fallen and have arisen, that are low and exalted, comely and ill-favored, fortunate and unfortunate, and he doth recognize that creatures follow the destiny of their deeds. And in sooth, sirs, those creatures that are attended by evil actions of body, word and thought, who speak evil of the noble ones, and are heretical in belief, and who share the evil consequences of heretical belief—they, after the dissolution of the body after death, attain punishment, misfortune, torture, and perdition. But, sirs, those creatures that are attended by good actions of body, word and thought, who speak no evil of the noble ones, and are right in their belief, and who share the (good) consequences of right belief—they, after the dissolution of the body after death, attain felicity and the heaven-world (*sagga-loka-*). Thus by his divine vision which is pure and transcending what is human, he doth recognize that creatures follow the destiny of their deeds. This, O monks, is the second knowledge attained by him; ignorance is destroyed and knowledge ariseth; darkness is destroyed and light ariseth, since he doth live ardent and resolute in mind, not disregarding Him.

'And furthermore, O monks, by the destruction of his Taints even in the world, a monk hath gained insight into the taintless Emancipation of Thought and Wisdom, and doth live (having) himself known and seen them face to face. This, O monks, is the third knowledge attained by him; ignorance is destroyed and knowledge ariseth; darkness is destroyed and light ariseth, since he doth live ardent and resolute in mind, not disregarding Him. Thus by the Law, O monks, do I account to be a brahman him that hath threefold knowledge, and no one else that merely talketh talk.'

To this effect spake the Blessed One, and hereupon said the following:

'Whoso knoweth his former abode,

[1] For another passage on previous existences compare § 22 of this work.

And heaven and punishment—
Him do I account to be a brahman
And no one else that merely talketh talk.[1]

Whoso knoweth his former abode,
And seeth heaven and punishment,
And who hath attained destruction of Birth,
Is a seer endowed with Insight.

By means of these three knowledges
A brahman becometh possessed of threefold knowledge;
Him I call " three-knowledged,"
And no one else that merely talketh talk.'

Exactly to that effect was it spoken by the Blessed One, so I have heard.

[End of the] Fifth Chapter [*i. e.* of the third division]

Résumé 10

Pleasure (§ 90)[2]; lived (§ 91)[3]; a robe (§ 92);
Fire (§ 93)[4]; investigation (§ 94)[5];
Source (§ 95)[6]; Lust (§ 96)[7]; goodness (§ 97)[8];
Gift (§ 98)[9]; by the Law (§ 99)[10]; these ten.

(End of the Third Division)

[1] Consult note above on this section. This particular stanza is probably corrupt; it is found only in B and C. For similar phraseology, compare the Dhammapāda, verse 423.

[2] Note that the stem form *pasāda-* is used, instead of the plural, and also the omission of *agga-*, ' chief, highest.'

[3] Note that the past ptcpl. *jīvita-*, ' lived,' is used, and not the noun *jīvika-*, ' livelihood.'

[4] Note the use of the sing. instead of the plur.

[5] *upaparikkhayā-;* this is a manufactured form to suit the meter. The common expedient of giving the instrumental case is impossible here, as the final foot must be an iamb.

[6] Note the use of the sing. instead of the plur.

[7] Note the use of the stem form *kāma-*.

[8] We should rather expect *kalyāna-sīla-*, ' of good character,' instead of *kalyāna-*, ' goodness.'

[9] Note the use of the sing. instead of the plural.

[10] This instrumental case is taken literally from the text.

§ 100. This verily was said by the Blessed One, said by the Sanctified One, so I have heard.

'O monks, I am a brahman devoted to begging,[1] ever pure-handed,[2] wearing my final body, the incomparable Healer and Physician.[3] Ye are my offspring here, born from my mouth, spiritually born, created by the Law, spiritual heirs (*dāyāda-*), not material heirs.

'There are these two kinds of gifts, O monks, namely, material and spiritual gifts, and of these two, O monks, the higher is the latter.

'There are these two kinds of distribution, O monks, namely material and spiritual distribution, and of these two, O monks, the higher is the latter.

'There are these two forms of kindliness, O monks, namely, material and spiritual kindliness, and of these two, O monks, the higher is the latter.

'There are these two forms of sacrifice, O monks, namely, material and spiritual sacrifice, and of these two, O monks, the higher is the latter.'

To this effect spake the Blessed One, and hereupon said the following:

'He that hath freely offered spiritual sacrifice,
Namely, the Consummate One, compassionate to all beings,
Such a one as he creatures will honor as best of gods and men,
And as one that hath passed beyond Existence.'

Exactly to that effect was it spoken by the Blessed One, so I have heard.

§ 101. 'There are, O monks, these four (things) which, although small and easy to obtain, are beyond reproach.' 'What four?' 'A dusty heap of rags, O monks, is both small and easy to obtain and is beyond reproach. Broken morsels of food, O monks, are both small and easy to obtain and are beyond re-

---

[1] *yāca-yoga-*, lit. 'yoked to begging'; we should rather expect *yācana-yoga-*. Edmunds, who has translated this section in his *Buddhist and Christian Gospels*, p. 131, renders, I think wrongly, 'suitable to beg of.'

[2] *pāyata-pāni-;* Edmunds renders 'drinking pure drink.'

[3] *salla-katta-*, lit. 'pain-causer.'

proach. The root of a tree as a dwelling[1] is both small and easy
to obtain and is beyond reproach. Urine that has become foul-
smelling as a medicine,[2] O monks, is both small and easy to
obtain and is beyond reproach. Verily these four (things), O
monks, although small and easy to obtain, are beyond reproach.
Since, therefore, O monks, a monk is contented with what is
small and easy to obtain and beyond reproach, him I declare to
be a higher member of the devotees.'

> 'In the case of him that is contented with what is beyond
>   reproach,
> With what is small and easy to obtain,
> The matter of attention to his bed and his seat,
> To his clothing, food and drink,
> Is no obstacle to his thought,
> Nor is he hindered by the sight of them.
>
> And by that monk who is content and zealous
> There have been acquired
> Those Laws which are said to be
> In accordance with the state of a devotee.'

§ 102. 'I proclaim the destruction of the Taints, O monks, to
the one that knoweth and to the one that seeth, but not to the one
that knoweth not and seeth not. And what is Destruction of the
Taints, O monks, for him that knoweth and for him that seeth?
To know that " This is Misery " is the Destruction of the Taints
for the one that knoweth and for the one that seeth. To know
that " This is the Origin (samudaya-) of Misery " is the Destruction of the Taints for the one that knoweth and for the one
that seeth. To know that " This is the Cessation of Misery " is
the Destruction of the Taints for the one that knoweth and for
the one that seeth. To know that " This is the Way leading to
the Destruction of Misery " is the Destruction of the Taints for
the one that knoweth and for the one that seeth. Thus indeed, O

[1] Following MSS. D, E, M, P, Pa, which read senāsanam.
[2] Following MSS. D and E, which read bhesajjam.

monks, to the one that knoweth and to the one that seeth there
cometh Destruction of the Taints.'

'Of a novitiate-monk who is under disciplinary training,
And who is following in the Straight Path,
The first understanding lieth in Destruction;
From this (there cometh) higher knowledge.

From this (there cometh) the knowledge of Emancipation,
The highest understanding of Emancipation;
In Destruction there ariseth the understanding
That the Fetters are broken.

Not, however, by the slothful,
Nor by the undiscerning,
Is this Nirvāna to be reached,
Which is the Deliverance from all ties.'

§ 103. 'Whatsoever devotees or brahmans there are, O monks,
that do not correctly comprehend that " This is Misery " and do
not comprehend that " This is its Origin, its Cessation, (and) the
Way which leadeth to its Cessation "—not mine, O monks, are
those devotees or brahmans, nor are they esteemed as devotees
or brahmans among the devotees and brahmans, nor do they,
when old, live, having known by themselves face to face and
having attained in (this) seen world the objective of devotees
and the objective of brahmans.

'But whatsoever devotees or brahmans there are, O monks,
that do correctly comprehend that " This is Misery " and likewise
that " This is its Origin, its Cessation, and the Way that leadeth
to its Cessation "—mine in truth, O monks, are those devotees
and brahmans, and they are, moreover, esteemed as devotees and
brahmans among those that are devotees and brahmans, and, when
old, live, having known by themselves face to face and having attained in (this) seen world the objective of devotees and
the objective of brahmans.'

'They that do not comprehend Misery
And (atho) the origin of Misery

And where Misery
Cometh wholly to nought,

And who know not the Path
Leading to the stilling of Misery—
They, deprived of the Emancipation of thought
And of the Emancipation of wisdom,
Are not fit for making an end (of existence);
They verily undergo Birth and Old Age.

But they that do comprehend Misery
And the origin of Misery
And where Misery
Cometh wholly to nought,

And who know the Path
Leading to the stilling of Misery—
They, endowed with Emancipation of thought
And with Emancipation of wisdom,
Are fit for making an end (of existence);
They do not undergo Birth and Old Age.'

§ 104. 'Whatsoever monks are endowed with Character, are
endowed with Contemplation, are endowed with Wisdom, and
with Emancipation and the Vision that cometh from the understanding of Emancipation, O monks, (who are) givers of admoni-
tion, teachers, instructors, advisers, (who are) stimulating and
encouraging, competent expounders of the Good Law—I declare
that associating with such monks as these, O monks, is exceeding helpful, and so likewise the hearing, approaching, and attending upon such monks as these, as well as being mindful (of the
commands) of these monks, and also imitating them in renunciation.' 'Why is this?' 'Since by honoring and worshiping and
attending upon monks of such a character, (an individual),
though imperfect in the Attributes of his Character, goeth to
perfection of Devotion, and, though imperfect in the Attributes
of Wisdom, goeth to perfection of Devotion, and, though imperfect in the Attributes of Emancipation, goeth to perfection of

Devotion, and, though imperfect in the Wisdom that cometh from the understanding of Emancipation, goeth to perfection of Devotion.

' Monks of such a nature as these, O monks, are called " teachers, carriers of teaching, forsakers of strife, dispellers of darkness, givers of splendor, radiance, brightness, torch-bearers, givers of light, noble, men with eyes." '

> ' Those that have discrimination, namely,
> Those with devoted minds, noble,
> Those who live according to the Law—
> They, I say, have a position that doth cause rejoicing.

> They glorify the Good Law,
> They are givers of light and illumination,
> Givers of splendor and wise are they,
> Far-seeing, forsakers of strife.

> Wise men, through having heard their teaching,
> And through having right knowledge,
> And through Insight into the destruction of Birth,
> Do not attain Re-existence.'

§ 105. ' There are, O monks, these four (sources of) creation[1] of Thirst, whereby Thirst, being created, doth spring up within a monk.' ' What four?' ' Because of his dress, O monks, Thirst being created doth spring up within a monk; because of food received within his bowl, O monks, Thirst being created doth spring up within a monk; because of his bed and seat, O monks, Thirst being created doth spring up within a monk; because of repeated existence,[2] O monks, Thirst being created doth spring up within a monk. These verily, O monks, are the four (sources of) the creation of Thirst, which being created do spring up within a monk.'

> ' A man accompanied by Thirst
> Undergoeth transmigration for a long time

---

[1] *uppāda-*, lit. ' springing up, coming into being.'

[2] *itibhāvabhava-;* the *iti* at the beginning of this compound is evidently a gloss of *ittha-* in line c.

And doth not pass beyond transmigration
With its manifold existences (lit. such and other existences).

Thus having known the distressing origin
Of the Misery of Thirst,
A monk that is freed from Thirst and without Attachment
    (anādāna-),
Wandereth forth thoughtful as a recluse (pari-vraj-).'

§ 106.[1] 'Those are brahman-like families, O monks, in whose
exalted house[2] parents are honored by their children. Those
families are like unto the ancient divinities, O monks, in whose
exalted house parents are honored by their children. Those families, O monks, are like unto the ancient teachers, O monks, in
whose exalted house parents are honored by their children.
Those families are like unto the worshipful, O monks, in
whose exalted house parents are honored by their children. The
appellation of such parents, O monks, is "Brahmans." The appellation of such parents, O monks, is "Ancient Divinities."
The appellation of such parents, O monks, is "Ancient Teachers."
The appellation of such parents, O monks, is "Worshipful."'
'Why is this?' 'Exceeding helpful, O monks, are such parents
to their children; they cause success, they give nourishment,
(they are) guiders of this world.'

'Parents who have kindly feeling
    Toward their offspring, are called
"Brahmans," "Ancient Teachers,"
"Worthy of oblation from their children."

Therefore, moreover, a wise man should honor
And revere them, both with food and drink,
And with raiment, bed, ointment, and bath,
And by washing their feet.

[1] Compare Windisch's footnote on this section, giving a comparison with
the Aṅguttara Nikāya.

[2] ajjhāgāre; I compare this word with Skt. adhi, 'over, above,' and āgāra-,
'house, residence,' making a tatpuruṣa compound. See Whitney, Skt. Gram.,
§ 1263 a.

On account of this ministration
Unto his parents, him they praise
As " wise " e'en here (on earth) ;
When he hath gone hence, he doth rejoice in heaven.'

§ 107. 'Exceeding helpful to you, O monks, are brahman householders who present you with garments, offerings (*pinda-pāta-*), beds, seats, requisites for sickness, medicines, and utensils.   And ye verily, O monks, are exceeding helpful to the brahman householders, for ye point out to them the Law of their first, middle, and last good actions, and ye do proclaim unto them the life of Chastity, with its meaning and its characteristics, absolutely complete and perfect.   Thus by mutual reliance, O monks, a life of Chastity is lived for the sake of crossing the Flood (of earthly longings), and for the sake of properly making an end of Misery.'

' Both those with houses and those without houses,
Being mutually dependent upon each other,
Do exalt the Good Law,
Which is Security unsurpassed.

And from them that have houses the houseless
Receive clothes, requisites (for sickness),
Beds and seats,
Shelter and entertainment.

Through reliance, moreover, on the Auspicious One,
Both householders and those without houses
Have Faith in the Sanctified One
And meditate with noble wisdom.

Having here (on earth) fulfilled the Law,
The Path that leadeth to Felicity,
They rejoice within the world of the gods,
(For) they follow (lit. they lust) their Lusts,[1] and take joy
    therein.'

§ 108. 'Whatsoever monks are deceitful and obstinate, O

---

[1] *kāma-* is apparently here not used in the usual bad acceptation.

monks, are chatterers, wavering, proud,[1] not self-composed—
these are not my monks and they are departed, O monks, from
this Discipline (*vinaya*-) of the Law, and they do not attain
growth, increase, or development in the Discipline of the Law.[2]
But on the other hand, O monks, those monks that are not deceitful, not chatterers, steadfast, tractable, well-composed, verily
they are my monks; they have not departed from the Discipline
of the Law, and they have attained growth, increase, and development in the Discipline of the Law.'

> ' Deceitful, obstinate, chatterers, wavering,
>   Proud, not self-composed—
>   They increase not in the Law which is pointed out
>   By the Perfectly Enlightened One.
>
>   Not deceitful, not chatterers, steadfast,
>   Tractable, well-composed—
>   They verily increase in the Law which is pointed out
>   By the Perfectly Enlightened One.'

§ 109. ' Just as,[3] O monks, a man carried away by the flood of
a river of pleasant and delightful aspect—should a spectator on
the shore see him, he (the spectator) would say: " Ho there!
Why art thou carried away by the flood of this stream of pleasant and delightful aspect? For there is below there a lake with
waves, whirlpools, crocodiles, and demons! When thou hast

---

[1] *unnala-*, lit. ' with the stalk raised up.' D'Alwis renders ' evil-disposed,'
and Childers, *Pāli Dict.*, s. v., quotes the commentary on the Dhammapāda,
verse 52, where we read *tesam mananalam ukkhipitva curanena unnalānam*, ' to
them who are called *unnala* because they walk uplifting the reed of pride.'

[2] It will be noticed that out of the six evil attributes assigned to the monks
in this paragraph, only five are paralleled with an opposite signification of
goodness in the paragraph which follows. The one not so paralleled is *siṅgī-*,
lit. ' horned,' which I have rendered ' wavering,' assuming that the idea in
the mind of the writer is deviousness or crookedness of character. Notice
further the different order of words in the list of the corresponding good
qualities which follows.

[3] *seyyathā*, a word of uncertain etymology used to introduce a simile, or
comparison, which in this particular section begins with the sentence further
down, starting *upamā kho me*, ' this is my simile.' The word occurs also in
§§ 91 and 99. See Childers, *Pāli Dict.*, s. v.

gone into that lake, O man, thou wilt meet with death, or with misery which is merely death." Then, forsooth, that man, on hearing these words, O monks, would struggle against the flood with hands and feet.

'This simile, O monks, is made for the conveying of a meaning. And this is the meaning: "The flood of the river" is the designation of Thirst; "pleasant and delightful in aspect" is, allegorically, the designation of private dwellings; "a lake below" is the designation of the five bonds of sensual life[1]; "with waves" is the designation of the frenzy of anger; "with whirlpools" is the designation of the five varieties of Lust; "with crocodiles and demons" is the designation of womankind; "against the flood" is the designation of Separation (nekkhamma-); "struggling with hands and feet" is the designation of the exertion of one's strength; "the spectator standing on the shore" is the designation of the Consummate One, the Sanctified One, the Perfectly Enlightened One.'

'When one hath forsaken Lusts with their Misery,
Seeking after Security in future,[2]
Of right comprehension, with mind well emancipated,
One may, in just this wise, experience Emancipation.
He that is versed in the Veda, and liveth chastely,
Is called "a goer to the end of the world, one that hath crossed over."'

§ 110. 'If as he walketh, there ariseth in a monk the idea of Lust, or the idea of Malevolence, or the idea of Cruelty,[3] O monks, and if the monk yield to this, and doth not forsake nor dispel it, nor banish it to non-existence,[4] a monk of such a charac-

---

[1] orambhāgiya-, Skt. avara-, 'lower,' and bhāgya-, 'something to be divided, lot, portion.'

[2] āyatim; so I prefer to read, following S, taking it as acc. of time. Compare the Skt. āyati-. All other MSS. read āyati.

[3] Compare this section with a similar passage in § 87.

[4] anabhāva-; this word seems to be a double negative, being the same in meaning as abhāva-; compare the Greek ἀνάεδνος, and see *Vinaya Texts*, vol. 2, SBE. 17, page 113.

ter is called slothful, froward, constantly and continually indolent, deficient in strength.

' If as he is seated, there ariseth in a monk the idea of Lust, or the idea of Malevolence, or the idea of Cruelty, O monks, and if the monk yield to this, and doth not forsake or dispel it, nor banish it to non-existence—a monk of such a character is called slothful, froward, constantly and continually indolent, deficient in strength.

' If as he reclineth, there ariseth in a monk the idea of Lust, or the idea of Malevolence, or the idea of Cruelty, O monks, and if the monk yield to this, and doth not forsake or dispel it, nor banish it to non-existence—a monk of such a character is called slothful, froward, constantly and continually indolent, deficient in strength.

' (But) if as he walketh, there ariseth in a monk the idea of Lust, or the idea of Malevolence, or the idea of Cruelty, O monks, and if the monk doth not yield to this, but doth forsake and dispel it, and doth banish it to non-existence—a monk of such a character is called ardent, not froward, constantly and continually strenuous, intent in mind.

' (But) if as he standeth, there ariseth in a monk the idea of Lust, or the idea of Malevolence, or the idea of Cruelty, O monks, and if the monk doth not yield to this, but doth forsake and dispel it, and doth banish it to non-existence—a monk of such a character is called ardent, not froward, constantly and continually strenuous, intent in mind.

' (But) if as he is seated, there ariseth in a monk the idea of Lust, or the idea of Malevolence, or the idea of Cruelty, O monks, and if the monk doth not yield to this, but doth forsake and dispel it, and doth banish it to non-existence—a monk of such character is called ardent, not froward, constantly and continually strenuous, intent in mind.

' (But) if as he reclineth, there ariseth in a monk the idea of Lust, or the idea of Malevolence, or the idea of Cruelty, O monks, and if the monk doth not accept this, but doth forsake and dispel it, and doth banish it to non-existence—a monk of such a charac-

ter is called ardent, not froward, constantly and continually strenuous, intend in mind.'

'If while either walking or standing,
   Or while sitting or reclining,
   A monk doth reflect upon an idea
   Which is evil or connected with household life (*gehanissita-*),

Having entered upon the path that is evil,
   And having become infatuated with Delusion—
   Such a monk as this is not able
   To experience Supreme Enlightenment.

But if, while either walking or standing,
   Or while sitting or reclining,
   A monk doth have control over his ideas,
   And is delighted by the quiescence (*upasama-*) of his ideas—
   Such a monk as this is able
   To experience Supreme Enlightenment.'

§ 111. 'Do ye live, O monks, endowed with Character; do ye
live endowed with the Precepts,[1] restrained by the restraint of the
Precepts, endowed with a wide range of good behavior, seeing
danger in the smallest faults, and do ye exercise yourselves in
the Subjects of Study, having taken them upon yourselves.   What
would be, O monks, the higher duty of monks living endowed
with Character, endowed with the Precepts, endowed with a wide
range of good behavior, seeing danger in the smallest faults, and
who exercise themselves in the Subjects of Study, having taken
them upon themselves?   If, moreover, while he walketh, a monk
hath become devoid of Covetousness, and likewise of Malevolence, Sloth, Torpor, Vanity,[2] and Moroseness, and hath got the
best of vacillation, his strength when exerted becometh unfailing,
his ready memory becometh not dulled, his body in repose is not
exerted, his thoughts are composed and collected; a monk of
such a character, O monks, even while walking, is called "ardent,

---

[1] See page 113, note 2.
[2] *uddhacca-kukkucca-*, Skt. *auddhatya-kaukatya-*.

not froward, constantly and continually strenuous, intent in mind."

'And if, moreover, while he standeth, a monk hath become devoid of Covetousness, and likewise of Malevolence, Sloth, Torpor, Vanity, and Moroseness, and hath got the best of vacillation, his strength when exerted becometh unfailing, his ready memory becometh not dulled, his body in repose is not exerted, his thoughts are composed and collected; a monk of such a character, O monks, even while standing, is called " ardent, not froward, constantly and continually strenuous, intent in mind."

'And if, moreover, while he is seated, a monk hath become devoid of Covetousness, and likewise of Malevolence, Sloth, Torpor, Vanity, and Moroseness, and hath got the best of vacillation, his strength when exerted becometh unfailing, his ready memory becometh not dulled, his body in repose is not exerted, his thoughts are composed and collected; a monk of such a character, O monks, even while being seated, is called " ardent, not froward, constantly and continually strenuous, intent in mind."

'And if, moreover, while he reclineth wakeful, a monk hath become devoid of Covetousness, and likewise of Malevolence, Sloth, Torpor, Vanity, and Moroseness, and hath got the best of vacillation, his strength when exerted becometh unfailing, his ready memory becometh not dulled, his body in repose is not exerted, his thoughts are composed and collected; a monk of such a character, O monks, even while reclining, is called " ardent, not froward, constantly and continually strenuous, intent in mind." '

'A monk should walk and stand restrainedly,
Should sit and recline restrainedly,
Should bend (his limbs) restrainedly
And should stretch himself[1] restrainedly

Upwards, across, and sideways.
Just as the course of the universe (*jagat-*) is regarded,
So is the rise and decay[2]

[1] I take *enam* reflexively, although I can find no parallel of such usage in Pāli or in Sanskrit.
[2] The same doublet occurs in Dhp., verses 113, 374.

Of the Attributes of things.

Such a monk, living in this wise,
Being ardent, reposeful in manner,
Not vaunting himself (lit. not puffed up)
With propriety and tranquillity of soul,
Ever mindful of his Subjects of Study—
Him they call " Constantly intent in mind." '

§ 112. This verily was said by the Blessed One, said by the
Sanctified One, so I have heard.

' The world, O monks, hath been thoroughly understood by the
Consummate One (tathāgata-) ; from the world the Consummate
One is wholly detached; the Origin of the world, O monks, hath
been thoroughly understood by the Consummate One, and it hath
been cast aside (pahīna) by him;[1] the Cessation of the world, O
monks, hath been thoroughly understood by the Consummate One,
and it hath been realized [2] by him; the Way leading to the Cessation of the world, O monks, hath been thoroughly understood by
the Consummate One, and hath been attained by him.

' Whatever, O monks, hath been heard, thought,[3] felt, obtained,
sought, pondered on in the mind, about the world with its gods,
its Māra (the tempter), its brahma, its race of devotees and brahmans—since (all) this is thoroughly understood by the Consummate One, for that reason he is called Consummate.

' (Between) the night, O monks, in which the Consummate
One obtained Incomparable Supreme Enlightenment, and the
night in which he obtaineth Complete Nirvāna (parinibbāna-)
through the element of Nirvāna which hath no Substrata remaining—all that which he speaketh, uttereth, and declareth cometh

[1] A genitive case used apparently with the force of an instrumental.

[2] sacchikaroti; this verb is translated in Childers, Pāli Dict., s. v., ' to bring
before one's eyes, to experience.' I should compare it with the Skt. sakṣi-kṛ-,
which Böhtlingk and Roth render ' zum Zeugen anrufen.' In Neumann, Bud-
dhistische Anthologie, p. 235, this whole section is translated, and this particular word is rendered ' verwirklicht.'

[3] muta-, participle of the verb munati, Skt. man-. For change of a to u,
Franke, Pāli und Sanskrit, p. 103.

absolutely to pass (and) it cometh to pass just so and not otherwise; for that reason he is called Consummate.

‘ Just as the Consummate One speaketh, O monks, so he doeth;
just as the Consummate One doeth, so he speaketh; inasmuch as
he doeth as he speaketh and speaketh as he doeth, for that reason
he is called Consummate.   In the world, O monks, with its gods,
its Māra, its brahma, its race of devotees and brahmans, the Consummate is surpassing, unsurpassed, comprehending the purposes
of others,[1] all-powerful—therefore is he called Consummate.’

To this effect spake the Blessed One, and hereupon said the
following:

‘ Having Insight into all the world,
Into all the worlds exactly,
Detached from all the world,
In all the world without compare—

All-surpassing in everything, steadfast,
Freed from all ties,
The highest Repose belongeth to him
Having attained Nirvāna, with no fear from any side.

This Enlightened One, with Taints destroyed,
Scatheless (anīgha-), having severed (the bonds) of doubt,
Hath attained destruction of all actions (kamma-)
(And) is released from the destruction of the Substrata.

This same Blessed and Enlightened One,
This lion beyond compare,
Hath set the Wheel of Brahma in motion
For the world with its gods—”.

Thinking this, the gods and men
Who have gone to Buddha for refuge,
Will worship him, after going,
As “ The Great One that hath transcended Time,

The Victorious One, best of those victorious,
Reposeful, Sage of those reposeful.

[1] aññadatthudasa-; see the note on this word, page 35, note 6.

Emancipated, highest of those emancipated,
The One that hath crossed, best of those that have
crossed—".

Thinking this they will worship him
As " The Great One that hath transcended Time ";
Nor is there in the world with its gods
'Any One thy equal.'

Exactly to this effect was it spoken by the Blessed One, so I
have heard.

End of Part Four

Résumé 11

After brahman (§ 100); four (§ 101); knowing (§ 102)[1];
Devotee (§ 103); Character (§ 104); Thirst (§ 105); brahman
(§ 106)[2];
Exceeding helpful (§ 107); deceit (§ 108)[3]; men (§ 109)[4];
Walking (§ 110); possessed of (§ 111)[5]; by the world (§ 112)[6];
these ten.

[End of] the hundred and twelfth section of the Iti-vuttaka

END OF THE ITI-VUTTAKA

---

[1] Present participle instead of the past participle.
[2] We should expect *sabrahmaka* of the text.
[3] Note the use of the noun instead of the adjective.
[4] Note the plural instead of the singular in the text.
[5] The important noun of the text, *sila-*, which is modified by *sampanna-*,
' possessed of,' is not given.
[6] Note the use of the instrumental case instead of the nominative, on
account of the meter.

ENGLISH INDEX

(The numbers refer to pages. Cardinal Buddhistic terms are given with their Pāli equivalents)

A

Actions painful to Buddha, 45
Actions not painful to Buddha, 45
Advantage, ānisaṃsa-, 48, 59
Aggregates, the, saṃkhāra-, 81, 99
All, the, sabba-, 24
Anger, khoda-, 3, 23, 27
Arrangement of the Iti-vuttaka, 1
Arrow, simile of the, 87
Association, sahavāsa-, 87
Association, or contact, saṃsagga-, 90
Attachment, anādāna-, 124
Attributes, khanda-, 29, 70, 122, 131

B

Belief, diṭṭhi-, 46, 62, 63, 79, 80, 81
Birth, 52, 54, 111
Body, the, 56
Brahma, 35, 78
Brahmans and devotees, 121
Brahman householders, 3, 125
Buddhaghosa, 2

C

Capitalization of cardinal words, 18
Caste (?), vanna-, 107
Cessation, nirodha-, 81, 82, 106, 120, 121, 131
Chain of Causation, paṭicca-samup-panna-, 81
Character, sīla-, 46, 70, 71, 87, 98, 114, 129
Charity, dāna-, 3, 35, 38, 39, 71, 85, 86
Chastity, brahmacariya-, 48, 62, 67, 68, 97, 98, 125
Cheerful, pamudita-, 60

Chief possession, the, 115
Clinging to existence, 94
Complete Nirvāna, parinibbāna-, 131
Connection between sections, 6
Consideration, vitakka-, 92
Construction of the Iti-vuttaka, 7
Consummate One, a glorification of, 131, 132, 133
Contact, saṃsagga-, 90
Contemplation, samādhi-, 70, 71, 94, 106
Covetousness, abhijjhā-, 129, 130
Craving, esana-, 67, 68
Cruelty, vihiṃsa-, 101, 127, 128

D

Death, 60
Decrease, parihāna-, 59
Deliverance, nissarana-, 81
Delusion, moha-, 22, 27, 28, 29, 64, 77, 78, 102, 103, 110, 111, 129
Desire, lobha-, 21, 25, 53, 54, 64, 102
Detachment from the world, 114
Deterioration in a monk's character, 90
Devadatta, the arch-sinner, 103, 104
Devotion, bhāvana-, 71, 94, 114, 122
Dialogue form of the Iti-vuttaka, 9
Difficulties of translation, 18
Discernment, vipassana-, 21–28, 58
Discipline, vinaya-, 114
Discrimination, nibbedha-, 54
Distribution, material and spiritual, 115, 119

E

Eightfold Path, the, 37, 106
Element, dhātu-, 56, 58, 81, 82, 99

PĀLI INDEX

(The numbers refer to pages. Where reference is made to notes, the English equivalent is not given)

A

akuppa-, genuine, 73
akusala-, impropriety, 64
akkheyya-, 74 n. 6
agamissa-, 55 n. 2
agga-pasāda-, 105 n. 6
ajjhagā, 89 n. 2
ajjhattam, 58 n. 2
ajjhāgāre, 124 n. 2
ajjhāvasati, 95 n. 1
aññathatta-, 31 n. 1
aññadatthadasa, 35 n. 6; 132 n. 1
a ñā-, knowledge, 73
aññātāvindriyaṃ, 73 n. 3
attiyamāna-, 63 n. 1
ati-, anu-, ava-jāta-, 83 n. 1
atipāta-, 83 n. 2
atidhāvanti, 62 n. 2
atekiccha-, 103 n. 2
atta-, soul, 106
adīnava-, transgression, 29
aduṭṭha-, 104 n. 6
addha-, 74 n. 3
adhi-gahetvā, 40 n. 2
anattha-, unseemliness, 102
anabhāva-, 127 n. 4
anavaññatti, 92 n. 3
anāgāmitā, not-returning, 21 n. 1; 59
anādāna-, attachment, 124
anāsava-, taintless, 65 n. 2; 77, 114
anītihaṃ, 48 n. 2
anuddayatā-, 92 n. 4
anupariyagā, 41 n. 1
anusaya-, inclination, 99
antarā āpādi, 103 n. 5
apāya-, 61 n. 3
appamāda-, zeal, 36 n. 4; 59

abyābajjha-, non-injury, 51 n. 4
abhabba-, predestined, 59
abhijjā-, covetousness, 129
abhijjhālū, 109 n. 2
abhiññā-, insight, 48, 49, 67, 81, 100, 123, 132
abhinivajjetvā, 100 n. 2
abhilāpa-, 107 n. 2
amattaññutā-, 43 n. 4
avijjā-, ignorance, 53, 69, 78
asaṃhīrā, 96 n. 2

Ā

āgantāro, 25 n. 2
ānāpāna-, inhalation and exhalation, 99
ānisaṃsā-, advantage, 48, 59 n. 2
āpajja-, 104 n. 3
āsava-, taint, 7, 52, 65, 69, 76, 77, 82, 98, 113, 114, 117, 120, 132
āyatiṃ, 127 n. 2
āhāra-netti, 56 n. 3, 58 n. 1.

I

icchā-, longing, 53
itibhavābhava-, 123 n. 2
idaṃ, 54 n. 1
indriya-, faculty, 36, 71 n. 4; 73 n. 5
imāya kampāya, 97 n. 2

U

uttama-attha-, Summum Bonum, 30
utthāna-, 86 n. 6
uddāna, 4, 5, 6, 26, 33, 42, 43, 50, 51, 64, 71, 79, 91, 92, 105, 118, 133

L

lapita-lāpana-mattena, 116 n. 1
lābha-, gain, 92
luddhāse, vedic plural, 21 n. 4
lobha-, desire, 21, 25, 53, 54, 64, 102

V

vacana-, the Word, 53
vaṭṭum, 106 n. 1
vatthu-, essential, 71
vadaññū, 84 n. 1
vanatha-, 90 n. 1
vanna-, caste (?), 107 n. 1
vasika-, 107 n. 3
vicikicchā-, moroseness, 129, 130
vijjā-, sapience, 99
viññāna, intellection, 88 n. 8; 111
vitakka-, 51 n. 3; 92 n. 2
vinaya-, discipline, 114
vipariṇāma-, law of transformation, 88
vipassana-, 58 n. 4; 60 n. 1
vipassin-, (creature of) discernment, 21 n. 3; 25, 26, 27
vimutti-, emancipation, 40, 59, 60, 114, 122
vimokkha-, release, 75, 95
virāga-, serenity, 106, 107
viveka-, seclusion, 52
vedana-, feeling, 7, 66
vedayitāni, 57 n. 4
veyyakaranāya, 100 n. 1
vyāpāda-, malevolence, 101, 107, 127, 128, 129, 130
vivattayi, 67 n. 1

S

samyojana-, fetters, 31, 38, 41, 48, 73, 92, 121
samvara-, restraint, 48
samvega-, 50 n. 2
samvejana-, 50 n. 1
samsagga-, contact, association, 90
samsāra-, transmigration, 29, 37 111
sakkāra-, one's own affairs, 48 n. 1; 92, 93, 94

samkhāra-, aggregates, 81, 99
samkhāya-, 75 n. 2
saṅgha-, 92 n. 5
samkiya-, 87 n. 1
saññama-, self-control, 35
sacchikaroti, 131 n. 2
sannino, 74 n. 5
saddhā-, faith, 96, 106
santi-, repose, 73, 100, 101, 110, 132
sabba-, the All, 6, 24
sama-, 79 n. 9
samacariya-, tranquil behavior, 36, 72
samatha-, tranquility, 99
samayam, 100 n. 4
samādhi-, contemplation, 70, 71, 94, 106
samadhigayha-, 36 n. 3
samussaya-, a mass, 68
sampajāna-musāvāda-, intentional falsehood, 38
sammaddasa-, proper vision, 81
sammāpāsam, 41 n. 3
sayam abhiññāya-, 114 n. 2
salla-katta-, 119
sallato, from its pang, 66
sa-vāhana-, 74 n. 1
sahavāsa-, association, 87
sahavyatam, 96 n. 1
sāra-, quintessence, 59
sikkha-pada-, subjects of study, 114, 129
siloka-, reputation, 48, 92
sīta-, 57 n. 5
sīla, sīlavat-, 46, 70, 71, 87, 98, 114, 129
sukha-, happiness, 71, 72
sukhuma-, subtle, 94
suññāgārānam, 59 n. 1
suppatiṭṭhita-, 95 n. 3
suppavedite, 96 n. 4
su-bhāvita-, 71 n. 1
subhikkhavāca-, 86 n. 2
sekkha-, 29 n. 4; 30
sevī-, 75 n. 1
seyyathā, 108 n. 5; 116 n. 2; 125 n. 3
socceyya-, 76 n. 1

THE COLUMBIA UNIVERSITY PRESS

COLUMBIA UNIVERSITY

INDO-IRANIAN SERIES

Edited by A. V. WILLIAMS JACKSON

Professor of Indo-Iranian Languages in Columbia University

Volume 1. **A Sanskrit Grammar for Beginners.** With Graded Exercises, Notes, and Vocabulary. By A. V. WILLIAMS JACKSON. *In preparation.*

The aim of this work is a practical one ; it is designed to furnish a book for the study of the classical Sanskrit in American and English colleges and universities.

Volume 2. **Indo-Iranian Phonology,** with Special Reference to the Middle and New Indo-Iranian Languages. By LOUIS H. GRAY, Ph.D., sometime Fellow in Indo-Iranian Languages in Columbia University. New York, 1902.

Cloth, 8vo, pp. xvii + 264, $2.00.

A brief statement of the phonetic developments undergone by the principal Indo-Iranian languages from the Sanskrit, Avestan, and Old Persian through the Pali, the Prakrits, and Pahlavi down to the Hindi, Singhalese, New Persian, Afghan, and other Indo-Iranian dialects. Special pains have been taken to make the work as convenient as possible for reference.

Volume 3. **A Bibliography of the Sanskrit Drama,** with an Introductory Sketch of the Dramatic Literature of India. By MONTGOMERY SCHUYLER, JR., A.M., sometime Fellow in Indo-Iranian Languages in Columbia University. New York, 1906.

Cloth, 8vo, pp. xi + 105, $1.50.

The design of this bibliography is to give as complete a list as possible of all printed and manuscript Sanskrit plays and of articles and works relating to the Hindu drama. The introduction furnishes a convenient epitome of the whole subject.

Volume 4. **An Index Verborum of the Fragments of the Avesta.** By MONTGOMERY SCHUYLER, JR., A.M. New York, 1901.

Cloth, 8vo, pp. xiv + 106, $1.50.

This index collects and cites all examples of each word found in the hitherto discovered fragments not included in Geldner's edition of the Avesta.

Volume 5. **Sayings of Buddha : the Iti-vuttaka,** a Pāli work of the Buddhist canon, for the first time translated, with introduction and notes. By JUSTIN HARTLEY MOORE, A.M., Ph.D. (Columbia), Instructor in French in the College of the City of New York. New York, 1908.

Cloth, 8vo, pp. xiii + 142, $1.50.

This volume presents a Buddhistic work not hitherto accessible in translation. The introduction treats of the composition and general character of the work and the chief features of its style and language. A full index of cardinal words facilitates cross-reference to the various sections.

Volume 6. **The Nyaishes, or Zoroastrian Litanies.** Avestan text with the Pahlavi, Sanskrit, Persian, and Gujarati versions, edited together and translated, with notes. (Khordah Avesta, Part I.) By MANECKJI NUSSERVANJI DHALLA, A.M., Ph.D. New York, 1908. Cloth, 8vo, pp. xxii + 235, $2.00.

The Pahlavi text, here edited and translated for the first time, is the result of a collation of seventeen manuscripts and forms an addition to the existing fund of Pahlavi literature. The introduction gives an account of the MS. material and discusses the relation of the various versions, their characteristics, and their value.

In addition to the Sanskrit Grammar for Beginners, the following volumes are also in preparation:

Priyadarśikā, a Hindu Drama ascribed to King Harsha. Translated from the Sanskrit and Prakrit by G. K. NARIMAN and A. V. WILLIAMS JACKSON, with notes and an introduction by the latter.

This romantic drama on the adventures of a lost princess was supposedly written by Harsha, king of Northern India in the seventh century, and is now to be published for the first time in English translation. Besides giving an account of the life and times of the author, the introduction will deal also with the literary, linguistic, and archæological aspects of the play.

Vāsavadattā, a Sanskrit Romance by Subandhu. Translated with an introduction and notes by LOUIS H. GRAY, PH.D.

This romance is one of the best examples of the artificial and ornate style in Sanskrit prose. Besides the translation, the volume will also contain the transliterated text of the 'South Indian' recension, which differs to a noteworthy degree from that of Hall, and a bibliography. The relation of the Sanskrit romance to the Occidental, especially the Greek, will be discussed in the introduction; and the notes will include parallels of incident in modern Indian and other folk-tales, as well as points of resemblance with other Sanskrit romances.

Daśarūpa, a treatise on Hindu Dramaturgy by Dhanaṃjaya. Now first translated, with the text and an introduction and notes, by GEORGE C. O. HAAS, A.M., sometime Fellow in Indo-Iranian Languages in Columbia University.

This work, composed at the court of King Munja of Mālava in the latter half of the tenth century, is one of the three most important treatises on the canons of dramatic composition in early India, a full discussion of which will be given in the introduction. The notes will contain important matter from the native commentary and references to parallel passages in the other treatises on dramatics and rhetoric.

Yashts, or Hymns of Praise, from the Khordah Avesta. Avestan text with the Pahlavi, Sanskrit, Persian, and Gujarati versions, edited together and translated, with notes, by MANECKJI NUS-SERVANJI DHALLA, A.M., Ph.D.

This volume is a continuation of the edition of the Khordah Avesta begun with the Nyaishes in volume 6 of the series and will be uniform with that volume in plan and arrangement.

Tales of the Dead: the Petavatthu, translated from the original Pāli, with introduction and notes, by JUSTIN HARTLEY MOORE, A.M., Ph.D.

The Petavatthu, one of the books of the Buddhist canon, has not hitherto been translated into any Occidental language. It contains material of interest in comparison with early Christian doctrines concerning hell. Reference will be made in the notes to the native commentary of Dhammapāla.

The following volume, not in the Indo-Iranian series, is also published by the Columbia University Press:

Zoroaster, the Prophet of Ancient Iran. By A. V. WILLIAMS JACKSON. New York, 1899.

Cloth, 8vo, pp. xxiii + 314, $3.00.

This work aims to collect in one volume all that is known about the great Iranian prophet. The story of the life and ministry of Zoroaster is told in twelve chapters, and these are followed by appendixes on explanations of Zoroaster's name, the date of the Prophet, Zoroastrian chronology, Zoroaster's native place and the scene of his ministry, and classical and other passages mentioning his name. A map and three illustrations accompany the volume.

THE COLUMBIA UNIVERSITY PRESS

THE MACMILLAN COMPANY, Agents

64-66 FIFTH AVENUE   NEW YORK

THIS BOOK IS DUE ON THE LAST DATE
STAMPED BELOW

AN INITIAL FINE OF 25 CENTS

WILL BE ASSESSED FOR FAILURE TO RETURN
THIS BOOK ON THE DATE DUE. THE PENALTY
WILL INCREASE TO 50 CENTS ON THE FOURTH
DAY AND TO $1.00 ON THE SEVENTH DAY
OVERDUE.

ND - #0024 - 140524 - C0 - 229/152/9 [11] - CB - 9781528269537 - Gloss Lamination